Abraham Lincoln's Ancestry:
German or English?

M. D. Learned's Investigatory History,
with an Appendix on Daniel Boone

Edited by

Don Heinrich Tolzmann

HERITAGE BOOKS
2016

HERITAGE BOOKS

AN IMPRINT OF HERITAGE BOOKS, INC.

Books, CDs, and more—Worldwide

For our listing of thousands of titles see our website
at
www.HeritageBooks.com

Published 2016 by
HERITAGE BOOKS, INC.
Publishing Division
5810 Ruatan Street
Berwyn Heights, Md. 20740

International Standard Book Numbers
Paperbound: 978-1-55613-754-9
Clothbound: 978-0-7884-5959-7

Contents:

Part One - Editor's Comments

In July 1992, I spoke at a meeting in Covington, Kentucky of the Kentucky German Heritage Society, which is headquartered in Louisville, on the topic of the state's German heritage. A member of the audience asked if I had ever heard that Lincoln may have been of German descent, and that the original spelling of the name may have been Linkhorn. I replied that I had not, but would investigate the matter. (1)

I became interested in the matter, as I had investigated a similar question as to whether Daniel Boone may have been of German descent, and whether the original spelling of his family's name may have been Bohne. My first step was to visit the birthplace and boyhood homes of Lincoln in Kentucky, which I then followed up with a search of the historical literature with regard to the question of Lincoln's ancestry.

I discovered that the real basis for the belief that Lincoln might have been of German descent was connected to Lincoln's grandfather, Abraham Linkhorn. This German spelling is overlooked in most sources, but when it is commented on, it is usually viewed as a mistake.

However, his grandfather apparently wrote his name in this manner in all documents, an indication that it was no one time mistake in writing. Not only had this grandfather written his name so that it appeared to be a German surname, his own gravestone, located in the Long Run Cemetery near Louisville, Kentucky, also carries the name "Linkhorn," which further demonstrates that this is the manner in which he wrote his name.

There is no question, therefore, that Lincoln's own grandfather spelled his name as would a German, however, this is not due to German heritage, but rather to the German influences the Lincoln family apparently absorbed by living in a region heavily populated by Rockingham County, Virginia Germans. Although the spelling of the name as "Linkhorn" displays definite German influence from the Virginia Germans, the family itself was not of German descent. However, the mere fact that Lincoln's grandfather spelled his name, as would a German, is an indication of the pervasive influence of the German element in Virginia. (2) Abraham Linkhorn's gravestone, therefore, is not only a monument to Lincoln's grandfather, but a material document testifying to the influence of the German heritage.

The spelling of the Lincoln name as Linkhorn obviously led to the question regarding his ancestry. In 1909, on the occasion of the centennial of Lincoln's birth, Prof. M.D. Learned, Chair of the German Department, University of Pennsylvania and editor of the venerable *German-American Annals*, published a monograph dealing with the question of whether or not Lincoln's family was of German descent. (3) This work contains the definitive answer to this question. It establishes without question that Lincoln was of English, not of German descent.

This work will be essential to all those who are interested in Abraham Lincoln, as well as to all those who are interested in Kentucky's German heritage. In Part Two, the investigatory history of Learned will be found, and in Part Three, the editor has included his research on Daniel Boone and the question of his ancestry having been German or English. I have included this, as it deals with some related matters of the influence of the German heritage.

The German-American interest in Lincoln derived not only from the possibility that he might have been of German descent, but also because Lincoln was one of the foremost U.S. Presidents, and especially because Lincoln had established such close affiliations and relationships with German-Americans. (4)

In the presidential campaign of 1860, Lincoln was strongly supported in his home state of Illinois by the foremost German-American spokesman there, Gustav Koerner, and Carl Schurz of Wisconsin would play a major role in the campaign after the Republican convention. (5) It is believed that German-Americans held the balance of votes in the following states: Missouri, Iowa, Minnesota, Illinois, Wisconsin, Indiana, Ohio, Michigan, Maryland, Pennsylvania, New Jersey, New York, and Connecticut.

Lincoln 's campaign was also strongly endorsed by the *Illinois Staats-Anzeiger*, edited by Theodor Canisius in Springfield, Illinois, which Lincoln had quietly purchased in May 1859. This enabled Lincoln's viewpoints on a whole variety of issues, especially Know Nothingism and slavery, to be explained to German-Americans, as well as to in effect provide German-American endorsement of Lincoln. (6)

The strong support Lincoln received from German-American voters was rewarded in numerous appointments. John George Nicolay was appointed as Lincoln's personal secretary.

Many received diplomatic posts: Canisuis was appointed as U.S. Consul to Vienna; Friedrich Hassaurek was appointed U.S. Minister to Ecuador; Charles N. Riotte became U.S. Minister to Costa Rica; Hermann Kriesmann became the Secretary of Legation to the Hohenzollern Court at Berlin; George E. Wiss was appointed U.S. Consul at Rotterdam; John P. Hatterscheidt became U.S. Consul to Moscow; Charles L. Bernays was appointed U.S. Consul at Zuerich; Henry Boernstein became U.S. Consul at Bremen; August L. Wolff was appointed U.S. Consul at Basel; August Alers was sent to Brunswick as U.S. Consul; and Francis J. Klauser became U.S. Consul at Amsterdam. Lincoln also made numerous federal appointments to German-Americans. There is no question that he was rewarding German-Americans via these appointments for the strong support they had given him in the 1860 election.(7)

In the Civil War, German-Americans were well represented, as one-fourth of the Union Army consisted of German-Americans. (8) Indeed, there were 5,000 German-born officers, of which 69 were from the upper ranks, which required appointment either by Lincoln, or the Secretary of War. (9) With regard to their Civil War service, Lincoln wrote "The Germans are true and patriotic." (10)

Given the strong interrelationships between Lincoln and German-Americans, it is not surprizing that the mere thought that Lincoln might have been of German descent caused such great interest. Since this question continues to be asked, the editor considered it important to edit this work for publication.

Notes

1. For a list of bibliographical references on the topic of Lincoln in German-American historical writing, see Don Heinrich Tolzmann, *Catalog of the German-Americana Collection, University of Cincinnati* (Muenchen: K.G. Saur, 1990), Vol. 1, pp. 136-49. A recent article on Lincoln noted that "He is the most written about figure in American history and the most mysterious..." See *U.S. News & World Reportt,* (5 October 1992).

2. For further information on the German element in Virginia, see the forthcoming volume, Don Heinrich Tolzmann, ed., *The German Element of Virginia: Hermann Schuricht's History*, (Bowie, Maryland: Heritage Books, Inc., forthcoming).

3. The volume originally appeared as: *Abraham Lincoln, An American Migration: Family English, Not German, With Photographic Illustrations* (Philadelphia: W.J. Campbell, 1909). I would especially like to express gratitude to Mrs. Erna Gwinn of Louisville with regard to the location of the cemetery where Abraham Lincoln's grandfather is buried.

4. For an overview of the relationships between Lincoln and the German-Americans, see Deny Brigance, "Like A Shout From the Watchtower of History: Abraham Lincoln and the German-Americans," Senior Paper, History Department, University of Cincinnati, 1992.

5. Regarding the 1860 election, see LaVern J. Rippley, *The German-Americans* (Boston: Twayne, 1976), p. 59.

6. With regard to Canisius, see A.E. Zucker, "Dr. Theodore Canisius, Friend of Lincoln," *American-German Review* 16:3(1950): 13-15, 38.

7. See Brigance, pp. 29-30.

8. Regarding Civil War service, see Rippley, pp. 58ff.

9. See Wilhelm Kaufmann, *Die Deutschen im amerikanischen Buergerkrieg* (Muenchen: R. Oldenbourg, 1911).

10. Cited in: Evarts B. Greene,"Gustav Koerner, A Typical German-American Leader: Address to the Seventh Annual Meeting of the German-American Historical Society of Illinois,"*Deutsch-Amerikanische Geschichtsblaetter* 7:2(1907): 82.

Part Two - Learned's History

TABLE OF CONTENTS

ILLUSTRATIONS

viii ILLUSTRATIONS

PREFACE

The following researches into the family of Abraham Lincoln, in America, are the outgrowth of a suggestion made by Dr. G. Langmann, of New York City, and were carried out by the encouragement which he gave. In 1901, Louis P. Hennighausen, Attorney-at-Law, in Baltimore, Maryland, published in the Report for the Society of the History of the Germans, in Maryland, an interesting article entitled "Abraham Lincoln or Linkhorn" supporting the view that Abraham Lincoln, the President of the United States, was descended from a German family by the name of Linkhorn. The argument was built up with much skill and found quite general acceptance among the Germans of America, giving rise to German poetry on Lincoln, the German President. In 1903, Dr. G. Langmann, wishing to have the question investigated in detail, requested the present writer to have some trained academic man from the University of Pennsylvania examine into the records of Lincoln's origin, and publish the results. Failing to find any one with sufficient time to devote to a thorough investigation of the subject, the present writer undertook the work himself. He examined all available records in the several states through which the Lincoln family migrated to Kentucky, namely Mass-

achusetts, New Jersey, Pennsylvania, Maryland,
Virginia, and that part of Transilvanian Virginia,
now known as Kentucky. In the course of the investigation, he unearthed and exploited much original matter relating to the Lincoln family in their
American wanderings.

The simple question of settling the name "Lincoln," or "Linkhorn," and its origin soon assumed
the more extended form of a study of the Lincoln
family as a *typical American migration*. It is this
two-fold form of the investigation which is published in the following pages.

The author wishes to express his indebtedness to
the following persons and institutions:

Former Governor S. W. Pennypacker, who allowed the author to make use of his rich collection of manuscripts; George F. Baer, President of
the Reading Railroad, who generously turned over
his notes on the Lincoln family in Berks County;
Louis Richards, President of the Berks County Historical Society, who gave access to his valuable
Note Books; B. F. Owen, of the Berks County
Historical Society, who assisted the writer in using
the Archives of the Society; Albert Cook Myers, of Moylan, Pa., for valuable assistance and
the Exeter cut; George C. Beekman, of Red Bank,
New Jersey, for information touching the Bownes
and Saltars of that state; Major Armour, of
Harrisburg, Pa., who allowed the author to use
the Account Books of John Harris; General John

E. Roller, of Harrisonburg, Virginia, who intro-
duced the author to the Lincolns in Rockingham
County, Virginia; Gilbert Cope, of West Chester,
Pa., who permitted the use of his valuable collection of Chester County papers; L. P. Hennighausen, of Baltimore, for information concerning the
Lincolns of Maryland and Loudoun County, Virginia; Colonel R. T. Durrett, of Louisville, Kentucky, who kindly furnished photographs of Lincoln documents; T. B. Fitzpatrick, of Hodgenville,
Kentucky, for the privilege of using photographs of
the Lincoln houses, published in his *Lincoln Souve-
nir*; the Librarians of the Historical Society of
Pennsylvania, the Historical Society of Virginia,
the Historic-Geneological Society of Massachusetts,
the State Library and Department of Public Records, Harrisburg, Pennsylvania; the Secretary and
his Assistant of the Department of Internal Affairs,
Harrisburg, Pennsylvania; the Office of Recorder
of Deeds, in Freehold, New Jersey, in Philadelphia,
West Chester, Reading and Lancaster, Pennsylvania, in Elkton, Maryland, and in Stanton, Harrisonburg and Winchester, Virginia, and also the
Office of the Secretary of State, Trenton, New
Jersey, and the Archives in the Surveyor's Office at
Perth Amboy, New Jersey.

The following members of the Lincoln family
have aided in furnishing information and giving
access to original materials:

Dr. J. E. Lincoln, Lacy Spring, Va.; Miss Kate

Pannebecker, of Linville, Va.; Mrs. Parvin (née Lincoln), of Leesport, Pa.; Mr. David Lincoln, of Birdsboro, Pa.; Mr. Richard Lincoln and Harrison G. Lincoln, and family, of Reading, Pa.; Mr. Francis H. Lincoln, of Boston, Mass.

As the aim of this study was not to furnish a family tree of the Lincolns in America, which task is being performed by the Geneologist, Mr. J. Henry Lea, the author of this work was happy to be able to turn over to Mr. Lea many of his geneological notes relating to the date of John Lincoln's migration to Virginia and the Lincoln epitaphs in the old graveyard on Linvill's Creek, for incorporation into Mr. Lea's *Ancestry of Abraham Lincoln,* and to receive in exchange some useful suggestions from Mr. Lea.

The documentary character of this investigation seemed to justify the printing of the most important deeds and other original papers in full. An effort has been made to give the exact text of these records in the original orthography. In some cases it was difficult to decide about the intended use of capitals in the originals, particularly in the case of the letters S and C, which were often written in such a way as to leave it doubtful whether the letters were intended to be large or small. Glaring mistakes in the original text are usually marked thus: [sic]

THE AUTHOR.

PHILADELPHIA,
THANKSGIVING DAY, 1908.

ABRAHAM LINCOLN

AN AMERICAN MIGRATION

Family English not German.

CHAPTER I.

THE LINCOLNS IN NEW ENGLAND AND NEW JERSEY.

As the Germans have given currency to the theory that Abraham Lincoln, the President of the United States, was of German ancestry and descended from a forebear by the name of "Linkhorn," in Pennsylvania, it has seemed worth while to test this theory in the light of the records of the Lincoln family. This study of the original documents relating to the Lincolns in the various significant centres of settlement in the colonial period makes it possible to follow the history of the migration of one of the most typical families in America and to trace the motives prompting the migration.

Abraham Lincoln, the President, knew very little about the history of his family, as is shown by a passage in a letter which he wrote, while a Member of Congress, in 1848, to Hon. Solomon Lincoln, of Hingham, Massachusetts: "My father's name is Thomas. My grandfather's was Abraham, the same as my own. My grandfather went from Rockingham County, Virginia, to Kentucky about the year 1782, and two years afterwards was killed by the Indians. We have a vague tradition that my grandfather went from Pennsylvania to Virginia, and that he was a Quaker. Further than this I have never heard anything. It may do no harm to say that 'Abraham' and 'Mordecai' are common names in the Lincoln family."

In an article contributed to Johnson's *Encyclopaedia* in 1859, Lincoln traces his ancestry, in a general way, back to New England. He had only a faint tradition of the connecting links in the migration of the various branches of the family from New England, and found the two chief arguments for his New England origin in the family tradition that they came from Massachusetts, and in the persistent recurrence of certain Christian names in the Lincoln family, as we have seen in the letter quoted above. This statement is particularly interesting, as it reflects the crude condition of American genealogy, even in the case of the family of a President of the United States, in the middle of the nineteenth century. This brief and indistinct outline of the Lincoln genealogy has been brought out into bold relief since the President's tragic death, and many missing links have been supplied by the genealogists, so that we are now in a position to trace with certainty the lineage of the great martyr President.

Even a decade later a biographer of Lincoln

writes the following concerning the residence of the Lincolns in Pennsylvania: "Where the Lincolns of Berks County (Pa.) came from, no records have as yet divulged, but they are believed to have been Quakers, and to have escaped from the intolerance of Massachusetts to the friendly soil of Pennsylvania." * Although this confession of ignorance on the part of the biographer appears to us now little less than naive, it is worthy of note, as this indifference and superficiality have not entirely disappeared from American biography.

The name Lincoln is clearly connected with the place and shire name "Lincoln" (Lind + Colonia) in England and is easily traced in the local records of Lincoln, as may be seen in the *Lincoln Marriage Licenses** recently published, in which are found the following entries:

"[a. 1612] John Lincoln of Witherne, yeom., aet 50, & ffaithe Cooke, of Libble Carlton, wid., aet. 34. appln. by Wm Hundleby, of Witherne, yeom.

[a. 1623] Rich. Lincoln of the Bail of Lincoln, yeom., aet. 28, & Susan Wood, of same Sp^r, aet. 26. appln. by ffrancis Walker, of same, yeom."

The researches of J. Henry Lea and J. R. Hutch-

---

* Cf. *Biographical Sketch of His Excellency, Lincoln, Late President of the United States. By Charles Henry Hart, LL. B.* (Reprinted from the Introduction to the *Bibliographia Lincolniana.* Albany, Joel Munsel, 1870, page 4.)

inson, in a forthcoming work, have traced the Lincolns back to Robert Lincoln in England, about 1540, in an unmistakable line leading down to the Lincolns of Hingham in England and of Hingham, Massachusetts, in New England.

THE LINCOLNS IN MASSACHUSETTS.

The history of the Lincolns, as we have it now from various sources, shows us that they came from Hingham in England and settled at and near Hingham, Massachusetts. The first settlement at Hingham, Massachusetts, was made by the Rev. Peter Hobart and twenty-nine others, who had land apportioned to them by lot September 18, 1735. The next year, 1736, lands were granted to the folfollowing Lincolns: Thomas Lincoln, the miller; Thomas Lincoln, the weaver, and Thomas Lincoln, the cooper. The following year, 1737, land was granted also to Samuel Lincoln, the brother of Thomas Lincoln, the weaver.**

Thomas Lincoln, the miller, was born in England in 1603, and died in Taunton, Massachusetts, in 1683. He first settled in Hingham, Massachusetts, and removed about 1652 to Taunton. He was called "the miller" to distinguish him from the other prominent Thomas Lincoln of Hingham, who was a large land owner and was known as Thomas Lincoln, the husbandman, thus making the fourth Thomas Lincoln who settled in Hingham. This Thomas Lincoln, the husbandman, came from Wyndham, England, in

---

** Cf. the articles on the Lincoln Family by Shackford and Egle, also Hart's *Biographical Sketch of His Excellency Lincoln.*

1638, and married about 1642 Margaret, the daughter of Richard Sanger, of Hingham. In addition to these four Thomases and Samuel Lincoln, two other Lincolns settled in the same region: Stephen Lincoln, the brother of Thomas Lincoln, the husbandman, and Daniel Lincoln.

Samuel Lincoln, who came over as a "servant" or apprentice, seems to have been the most modest of all the Lincolns in point of property. In the Office of Rolls in London is found the following reference to him: "Francis Lawes, born in Norwich, Norfolk County, and lining weaver, aged —, and Liddea, his wife, aged 49, with one child, Mary, and two servants: Samuel Lincoen, aged 18 years, and Ann Smith, aged 19 years—ar desirous to pass to New England to inhabit." These people went to New England with William Andrews, of Ipswich, Master of the ship John and Dorothy, of Ipswich, and William, his son, Mr. of the Rose of Yarmouth, April 18, 1637.* It was this Samuel Lincoln, the "servant," who by the irony of democracy became the progenitor of the family of Abraham Lincoln, the President of the United States of America. Samuel Lincoln thus came from Norwich, England, in the year 1637, at the age of 18 years. He died May 26, 1690. He married Martha (Lewis), who died April 10, 1693. Ten children were the issue of this union. The eldest son, Samuel, became the progenitor of Lincolns of prominence in Massa-

---

* Cf. *Chicago Tribune*, Apr. 14, 1883.

chusetts. The fourth son, Mordecai, was born June 17, 1657, in Hingham, and died October 13, 1727, in Scituate, Massachusetts.* This Mordecai was the great, great, great grandfather of Abraham Lincoln, the President. Mordecai Lincoln was a blacksmith by trade, and established the first smelting furnace in New England. He was a large contributor towards the erection of the Iron Works at Bound Brook, Massachusetts, which comprised as their chief feature a Catalan forge for making wrought iron.** There is record of him as a foot-soldier of Hingham, Massachusetts, in 1679, and as a blacksmith in Hull about 1680. In the years 1680 to 1685 he is found among the taxables and is assessed 2/4 Bull. for money there in 1684. His land, or residence, is mentioned in the deed given by Benjamin Bosworth and his wife, Beatrice, to Robert Gould Hull, December 14, 1682. His uncle, Thomas Lincoln, the weaver, appears as witness of a deed in 1698.***

A deed in the possession of George Lincoln, of Hingham, dated December 21, 1713, contains the

---

* Cf. *Chicago Tribune*, April 14, 1883. (Cp. *Cincinnati Gazette*, Oct. 6, 1882, referring to Mr. S. Bernard Elliott, of Pataskala, O., as having fixed the pedigree of President Lincoln.)

** Cf. James M. Swank, *History of the Manufacture of Iron in All Ages, and Particularly in the United States, from Colonial Times to 1891*. (Second Edition, Philadelphia, 1892, page 505.)

*** Cf. Ms. Notes on the Lincoln Family in the Massachusetts Hist. Genealogical Society, Boston.

following information: "George Jackson, of Marblehead, sells to Mordecai Lincoln, of Scituate, "blacksmith," two parcels of salt-meadow land lying and being in Cohassett, then the Township of Hingham, one of which is bounded East by a brook or river called Bound Brook."

Mordecai, the blacksmith, married Sarah, the daughter of Abraham and Sarah (Whitman) Jones. He moved first from Hingham to Hull, and about 1704 to the neighborhood of Scituate, where he built his furnace for smelting ore. Mordecai and Sarah Lincoln had the following children: Mordecai, Abraham, Isaac and Sarah—all born at Hingham, Massachusetts—and Elizabeth and Jacob, born at Scituate, Massachusetts. In 1727, Mordecai Lincoln, of Hull, willed his sons and executors, Isaac and Jacob, his real estate in Hingham and Scituate. To his other sons, Mordecai and Abraham, he gave 110 pounds and 160 pounds, respectively, in money and bills of credit. These were the sons, doubtless, who had gone to settle in Monmouth County, New Jersey, adjoining Middlesex, in which county (near Woodbridge) the Massachusetts families of Ilsleys, Moores, Hales, Rolfes, Pikes and others had settled.

It would appear that the Lincolns had found their way to New Jersey and Maryland before 1700. There is mention of Lincoln's Inn, Middlesex County, as early as April 5, 1685, and March 4, 1691-2, showing that the name was fresh in the minds of the early settlers. In Maryland a number of important entries, particularly in the land records of Cecil County, date back to the same early period. The following entry, for example, shows that there was already a tract of land in Cecil County, called by the name of "Linckhorne," after the manner of plantations in the South:

> Maryland Ss/ Know all men by these presents that wee Jonathan Linckhorne and Alexander M^{cc}Key [McKoy] of Cecell County planters have leased Lett Assigned & Sett over unto Wm Blay of ye Said County * * * * * tract called Linckhorne wch lies on ye East Side of ye Mill branch [for a term of 99 years from date (April 27, 1704). Consideration £5000 of tobacco].

Jonathan Linckhorn   (Seal)

his

Alex^r. M Mackey   (Seal)

mark

Witnesses:
  Wm Wilson
  Peter Allaby
    his
  Jno — Linckhorne
    mark

[Recorded August 16, 1704. Copied in unbound deed book pp. 188-189, Court House, Elkton, Maryland.]*

Wm. Lincolne appears among the witnesses of the will of Richard Wells, Sr., in Anne Arundel Co.,

---

* From the notes of Albert Cook Myers.

Md., June 22, 1667, and Anne and Jon. Lincoln as witnesses of the will of Nathaniel Garrett, Cecil Co., Md., Apr. 27, 1688.

It is worthy of note that the names Lincoln (or Linckhorne) and McCoy (or McKay), found together here in Maryland, and the names Lincoln (or Lincon) and Schenck (or Shanks), found together in New Jersey, are all met with again in the Valley of Virginia in the latter half of the eighteenth century.

THE LINCOLNS IN NEW JERSEY.

It cannot be reasonably questioned that Mordecai Lincoln and Abraham, his brother, of Monmouth County, New Jersey, were the two sons whom Mordecai Lincoln, of Hull, Massachusetts, mentioned in his will in 1727. The circumstantial evidence is quite convincing. First, the fact that the father gave the children at home his land, but to the two brothers, Mordecai and Abraham, their portion in cash, would indicate that they had gone away from home. Second, these two Lincolns, Mordecai and Abraham, are not found in any records of that period, except in those of Monmouth County, New Jersey. Third, these two brothers, Mordecai and Abraham, are found in New Jersey in a settlement made by New Englanders, largely from Massachusetts.

The exact date of the settlement of Mordecai and Abraham Lincoln in East Jersey has not been definitely determined. The earliest record of a Lincoln in New Jersey is a reference to Mordecai Lincoln found in the will of Captain John Bowne, a merchant of Middletown, New Jersey. The will is dated September the 14th, 1714, and shows that Mordecai Lincoln was already married to Hannah Saltar, daughter of Richard and Sarah (Bowne) Saltar, of Freehold, New Jersey, and was evidently settled there. In accordance with the terms of this will, John Bowne bequeathed to his niece, Hannah (Saltar) Lincoln, the sum of 250 pounds. The text of the will runs as follows:

In the Name of God Amen This fourteenth day of September in the year of Our Lord 1714,—I John Bowne of Midletown Merchant being sick and Weake in body but of perfect mind and memory thanks to God therefore but Calling to mind the Mortality of the body and that it is appointed [once] for all men once to die do make and ordain this my last Will and Testament; first and principally J give and bequeath my soul into the hands of God that gave it and my body J recommend to the Earth to be buried in a Christian like and decent Manner at the discretion of my Executors here after Named and as to my worldly Estate J give and dispose of the Same in manner following, Imprimus my Will is that all my Just debts be all paid and discharged; Item I give to my wife Frances Bowne the Sum of four hundred pounds money of the Province aforesaid in Right of her Dowry Jtem J give and bequeath to my Sister Sarah Saltar all my Plate and the bed whereon J lye and furniture. Jtem J give to Gersham Mot the the sum of two hundred pounds for the use of his Children. Jtem J give to Joseph Dennis one hundred and twenty pounds, to Ieremiah White the sum of one hundred and twenty pounds, Jtem to Thomas Saltar and John Saltar and Hannah Lincon and to William Hartshorn's three Eldest Chilldren the sum of two hundred and fifty pounds to each of them. The Rest of my Estate both Real, and Personall I Will to be Equally Divided between my Brother Obadiah Bowne and my Brother Richard Saltar, their Heirs and Assigns for Ever, Whome I do hereby appoint Sole Executors of this my last Will and Testament Jn witness whereof J have hereunto set my hand and Seal the day and year first above written.

John Bowne.

Signed, Sealed and Delivered
   in Presence of
   James Paul
   Joseph Dennis
   Marget Commen*

[Affidavits of witnesses & certificates of Ro. Hunter, Governor.]

Mordecai Lincoln is appears as "Mordecai Linhorn" among the mortgagors in the inventory of Capt. John Bowne's estate in 1714.

Another reference to Mordecai Lincoln in East

---

* Will of John Bowne Sept. 14, 1714, Recorded in A 10 & recorded with affidavits A 27, State House, Trenton.

New Jersey, is found in a letter of John Saltar to
his uncle, Obediah Bowne, executor of Captain John
Bowne, dated April 25th, 1716. The part of the letter in question runs as follows:

April 25th 1716.

Honord vncle Bowne

I have Sent by my father Such writings as were
in my hands & appurtaining to the Estate of my
dec^d vncle Capt John Bowne. Neare fifty pound
in them my vncle had given to me, not many
weeks before he dyed, & time failing the property
of the debt was not altered in my Name soe because I cannot fairly pretend to proceed to Secure myself w^thout yor loane [?] I have thought fit
to remitt ye same to ye Estate. Haueing onely an
order to take Security for the Same to my owne
use from vndr his hand & Soe Expect y^t yo will
be favorable to me on y^t Score; I depend on your
Courtesy y^t which was given to me is not in y^e
Inventary, I have alsoe Send a bond from John
Chenoath to my vncle vnder Such like Circum-
stances for ten pounds & not altered as was ordered & Intended to my brother Lincon—the
whole that is giuen and Secured to my brother
Thomas Mardden [Madden?] & my self amounts
in all to about four hundred & twenty pounds or
thereabouts * * * * * * * * * *

Yor Ever faithful & obedient Nephew,

John Saltar*

---

* This letter was found in 1907 in the possession of Mr.
William Crawford, near Red Bank, N. J., who allowed the
present writer to photograph it.

The importance of this letter for us is to be found in the fact that in it John Saltar calls Mordecai Lincoln, or Lincon, his brother, thus showing that Mordecai Lincoln's wife, Hannah Saltar, was John Saltar's sister, and so establishing an important family relation for the New Jersey record of the Lincolns.

The next trace which we have of Mordecai Lincoln in East Jersey appears in a law suit begun by Obediah Bowne in the Monmouth County court, in the year 1716, and continued for a period of four years. The brief minutes of this trial are still extant in the original manuscript *Court Book* in Freehold, New Jersey, and afford such an interesting glimpse into the Jersey court procedure of that early time that they seemed worthy of insertion here:

Court of Com Pleas Feb 28, 1716

Obadiah Bowne
  Adm^r &c

   u

Mordecaj Lincoln

Debt

£140

The Like Rule [Plaint. 20 Days to file Declar & Defend^t 20 Days to give in Special Bail & to Plead as the Law Directs] Nonsuit for Want of a Proper Power of Attorney.

Court Session May 35, 1717 (8 a. m.)

Obadiah Bowne
Administrator &c
u
Mordecaj Lincoln
Debt
£140

After hearing Mr. Vernon for yᵉ Plᵗ & Mr Gordon for the Defendᵗ Court allowed a Non Pros.

Court Aug 27, 1719

Obadiah Bowne Admʳ
u
Mordecaj Lincorn
Debt
£140 Non Est

Court 28 November 1719

Obadiah Bowne Admʳ
of Elis: Bowne Deced
u
Mordecaj Linckorn
Debt
£140 Non Est

Court May 27, 1720

Obadiah Bowne Admʳ
u
Mordecaj Lincon &
    Richard Saltar
Debt
£140

Mr. Kinsey P Pl^t Ordered that the Sherif Bring
ye Body That the Pl^t Declare Twenty Days The
Defend^t to Give Sp: Bail in the like Time.
Nonsuit to ye action u Saltar for Want of Letters adminis & Nonsuit to ye action u Lincon
for Want of a Declar.

Court Aug 27. 1720

Obadiah Bowne Adm^r
[u]
Mordecaj Lincon &
Richard Saltar
Debt
£140

Ordered that the Nonsuits in this action be set
aside that Lincon have Twenty Days time to give
Special Bail and that Each of them have Twenty
Days time to Plead, Mr. Kinsey to Declare against
Lincoln in the Same time upon Payment of costs
by Mr. Saltar the Action against Lincon With-
drawn by Consent of the Pl^t attorney.

In the jury which sat at the Court of Common
Pleas August 29, 1717, we find Mordecai Lincoln,
Jonathan Borden and Benjamin Borden.

Mordecai Lincoln appears also in another suit
brought by him against John Liming, November
the 30th, 1721, and continued until November 29th,
1722. The proceedure is briefly recorded in the
Court Book as follows, and shows that Mordecai
Lincoln, either in person or through his attorney,
transacted business in New Jersey at this time:

Court Nov. 30 1721

Mordecaj Lincon

u

John Liming

Debt

£.. 9.—Non est

Court Mar 1 1721

Mordecaj Lincon

u

John Liming

Debt

£11.. 9.—Non est

Court Nov. 29, 1722.

Mordecaj Lincon

u

John Liming

Debt   Mr. P. Plaintif

£11.. 9.. The Like Rule.

The last direct reference to Mordecai Lincoln as resident in New Jersey is found in the following deed issued by Richard Saltar to Mordecai Lincoln under date of February 2d, 1720:

This Indenture made this Second Day of February in ye Sixth year of his Majestys Reign King George &c over Great Brittain France and Ireland Defender of ye faith &c Annoq Domini one thousand seven hundred and twenty *Between* Richard Saltar of the Towne of freehold County of Monmouth and and [sic!] Province of New Jersey of ye one Party and Mordecai Lincon of of [sic!] ye Same of the other Party *Witnesseth* y^t ye said Richard Saltar for and in Consideration of ye sum of one hundred and and fifty two Pounds Curant Money of ye Province aforesaid to ye said Richard Saltar by ye s^d Lincon already in hand Paid the receipt whereof he ye said Richard Saltar Does hereby owne and that he is therewith fully Satisfyed and Paid and thereof and therefrom Does hereby fully clearly and absolutely aquit Release and Discharge ye said Mordecai Lincon his Heirs Exts & adm^s and every of them forever, HATH given granted Bargained sould aliened Enfeoffed Released and discharged and by these Presence Doth give grant Bargain Sell and Confirme unto him ye said Mordecai Lincon his heirs and assigns forever all those Tracts of Land & Meadow on Machaponix River & Gravill Brook in the County of Middlesex, the first Tract Is bounded on said Matchaponix River on ye South by ye Pine Brook East by the Land now or Late of Willm Estill on ye west, and by Land unsurveyed on ye North ALSO all that Tract Bounded westerly by Gravill Brook Southerly by the Land of William Estill from ye Mouth of Long Meadow Run Easterly & Northerly by Land unsurveyed. ALSO all ye Long Meadow. Upon ye s^d Long Meadow Run Bounded west by ye Last Mentioned Tract of Land and all round ye other side up Upland Unsurveyed In all containing four Hundred are. [acres] More or Less besides allowance for barron Land and High Ways with all the Royaltys Proffets advantages Hereditaments &

appurtenances to yᵉ said Land and Meadow Belonging or in anywise apertaining also all yᵉ Estate Right title Interest claime and Demand Wᵗsoever of yᵉ said Richard Saltar of in & to or out of yᵉ Same on any Part of them as amply and fully to all Intents & Purposes asyᵉ same ward [sic] conveyed and assured to him by a certain Deed of Sale Bearing Date yᵉ seventh Day of November Annoq Domini 1717 from John Reid Esquire TO HAVE AND TO HOLD yᵉ said Severall Tracts of Land and Premises with their appurtenances unto him yᵉ said Mordecai Lincon his heirs and assigns to yᵉ only Euse and behoof of yᵉ said Mordecai Lincon his heirs and assigns forever and the said Richard Saltar Doth for himself his heirs exˢ and admˢ to and with yᵉ said Mordecai Lincon his heirs and assigs [sic] Covenant Promise and agree In yᵉ Manner and forme following Viz: that the Granted and Bargained Premises with yᵉ appurtenances are free and Clear of Incumbrances and that yᵉ said Richard Saltar hath good Right full Power and Lawfull Authority to Sell and Confirme yᵉ Same In Manner aforesaid and yᵗ yᵉ said Richard Saltar his heirs Exˢ & Admˢ Shall and will forever warrant and Defend yᵉ Same In yᵉ Peacable and quiet Possession and Seizen of him the said Mordecai Lincon his heirs and assigns against all Persons whatsoever *In Witness* whereof the said Richard Saltar hath hereunto set his hand and Seale yᵉ day and year first above written.   Richard Saltar (S)

SEALED and DELIVERED In the Presence of Thomas Cox, R. Saltar Junʳ.

April 5, 1727 Then appeared before John Anderson Esqr one of his Magestys Councill for the Province of New Jersey Richard Saltar Junr a Subscribing Evidence to the above written Instrument who being Solemnly sworn on the Holy Evangelists of Almighty God did declare that he saw Richard Saltar therein Named Execute the same as his Act and Deed.

Exam^d by Thos Barrow Sec.

In the year 1728 in the inventory of Elizabeth Salter's Estate mention is made of a debt due Mordecai Lincon.*

NATHAN LINCOLN OF NEW JERSEY.

There is record in Sussex County, New Jersey, of another Lincoln, Nathan by name, whom we have not been able to trace elsewhere. The document in question is the will of Nathan Lincoln (or Linken) beginning and closing as follows:

"I, nathan Linken [Linkon?] of Sussex County & Westrin division of ye province of New Jersey
* * * * * * * * * * * * * * *
Signed, sealed, published pronounced & delivered by the sd Nathan Linken to be his last Will in presence of us
John Wood
    her
Mary [X] Young,
    mark
Brice Bicky."

* Cf. *New Jersey Archives*, First Series xxiii, p. 401.

The will is dated August 7th, 1763. It was recorded January 14th, 1767. By a strange mistake, the signature of the testator was misread as Nathan Metopon, instead of Nathan Linken, and was calendared under Metopon. It was only by accident that the present writer discovered the identity of this Metopon and thus discovered this third Jersey Lincoln. It lies beyond the purpose of this study to attempt to trace the relation of this Nathan Lincoln to Mordecai and Abraham of Monmouth County, New Jersey, on the one hand, or to the Maryland Lincolns on the other.

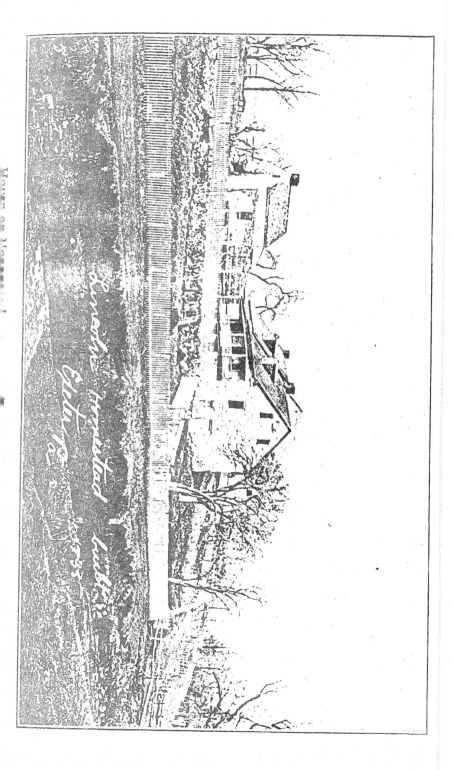

CHAPTER II.

THE LINCOLNS IN PENNSYLVANIA.

Both Mordecai Lincoln and his brother Abraham Lincoln migrated from New Jersey to Pennsylvania, where they spent the remainder of their lives, each rearing a numerous family. It is in Pennsylvania that we find the most abundant information of the Lincoln family. Scores of references to the Lincolns are still preserved in the land records of Harrisburg, Philadelphia, West Chester and Reading, as will appear in the documents printed below.

MORDECAI LINCOLN IN PENNSYLVANIA.

Mordecai Lincoln begins to appear in the Pennsylvania records in 1720 and we may suppose that he migrated from East Jersey to Pennsylvania some time, probably soon, after February 2nd of that year. In the old burying ground near Allentown, Pennsylvania, is found an epitaph which reads "To the Memory of Deborah Lincoln, Aged 3 yrs. 4 mos. May 15, 1720." This probably refers to a child of Mordecai and Hannah Lincoln. The name of Mordecai Lincoln is found in the tax lists of Chester County, Pennsylvania, in 1720 and the following years, as these extracts from the original lists will show:

1720 near ye Branches of the French Creek &
    Brandywine
      Mordecay Lncoln   3s. d.
1722 Nantmeal
      Mordecai Lincoln   2s. 6d.
1724 Coventry
      Mordecay LinColn   4s. 4d.
1725 Coventry
      Mordecay Lincolin   3s. d.

These tax lists show that Mordecai Lincoln was assessed both in the township of Nantmeal and in that of Coventry "near ye branches of the French Creek & Brandywine." We learn further particulars about his land in Coventry in another document entitled "Articles of Agreement" between Samuel Nut, William Branson and Mordecai Lincoln, dated February 28th, 1723:

    "Articles of Agreement Indented made and Concluded the Twenty Eighth Day of February Anno Doni 1723/4 Between Samuel Nut of the Township of Coventry upon the French Creek in Chester County Ironmonger of the first Part William Branson of the City of Phila. Merch^t. of the Second Part and Mordecai Lincoln of Coventry afores^d. Ironmonger of the Third Part In Manner following that is to say—
    Whereas The s^d Samuel Nut William Branson and Mordecai Lincoln Have at their Joint Charge lately erected Built and provided one Dwelling House and a Forge with Engines belonging to

their Iron Works besides other Buildings & Erections Situate Lying and being on a Certain Tract of Land at French Creek afores^d. * * * Articles of Agreement Indented made and Concluded the Twenty-eighth Day of February Anno Doni 1723 Between Samuel Nutt of the Township of Coventry upon the French Creek in Chester County Ironmonger of the first Part Mordecai Lincoln of Coventry afores^d. Ironmonger of the Second Part and William Branson of the City of Phila. Merch^t. of the third Part In Manner following that is to say—

Know all men by these Pres^s that I Mordecai Lincoln of Coventry In the County Chester for and in Consideration of the Sum of Five Hundred Pounds of Current Lawful Money of America to me in Hand paid by William Branson of Phila. Merch^t. The Receipt whereof I do hereby Acknowledge and thereof do Exonerate Acquit and for Ever Discharge the s^d William Branson his Heirs For Ever have bargained sold remised released and quitclaimed And by these Presents Do Bargain sell remise release and for Ever quit claim unto him the said William Branson his Heirs and Assigns for Ever all and Singular the one full undivided third Part of One Hundred Acres of Land as also one full undivided third Part of six Acres of Land Together with all my Right Title Interest and Claim whatsoever of in or to the afores^d undivided Rights according to Articles of Aggreem^t made Between Samuel Nutt of the one Part and Mordecai Lincoln of the other part Together with

all and Singular the Mynes and Minerals Forges
Building Houses Lands Improvements whatsoever
thereunto belonging or in any wise appertaining to
the only proper Use and Behoof of him the said
William Branson his Heirs and Assigns for Ever
IN WITNESS WHEREOF I have hereunto Set my
Hand and Seal the fourteenth Day of December.
1725   mordecai Lincoln
    Sealed & Delivered
In presence of
Jona Robeson
Jam Sheary*
    Recorded by John Kinsey Jan. 4 1744/5.

The next reference to Mordecai Lincoln in Pennsylvania is a deed of Richard Saltar to Mordecai
Lincoln, dated May 26th, 1726. In this deed Mordecai Lincoln is mentioned as "of the County of
Chester in the prov'ce of Pensilvania." The document runs as follows:

THIS INDENTURE WITNESSETH That Richard
Saltar of Frehold in the County of Monmouth
& Prov^ce of New Jersey Yeoman for and in Consideration of the full and Just sum of——pounds
in hand paid to the said Richard Saltar by Mordecai Lincon of the County of Chester in the
Prov^ce of Pensilvania the Rec^t whereof the
said Rich^d doth hereby Acknowledge and is therewith fully Satisfied Contented and paid & thereof

---

* Power of Attorney D. 2. v. 2, p. 370, Department of
Internal Affairs, Harrisburg, Pa.

and from every part & parcell thereof doth fully clearly and absolutely Aquit Exonerate and discharge him the said Mordecai Lincon his heirs and Assigns forever Hath granted Bargained and sould unto the said Mordecai Lincon his Heirs & assigns forever All that Tract of Land lying in the County of Midelsex in New Jersey aforesaid Beginning at a Black Oak Tree marked on four sides standing On the North side of a small slough or run wch is on the North side of a Farm formerly Wm Estell, from thence running North thirty nine degrees westerly Seventeen chains to Matchaponix River thence down the same to the Mouth of a Brook which is One of Robt Barclays Corners & running from the first mentioned Black Oak Tree att the Beginning South forty eight degrees Easterly forty chains more or less to the reere Lines of s^d Estills Farme thence along the same North & by East & half a point easterly to his corner where a small run comes into the brook thence down the Brook to the above named Barclays corner On Matchaponix River—Which Tract of Land by Estimation One Hundred Acres more or less. To Have and To Hold the said Tract of Land with the appurtenances and privileges to the same belonging or in any wise apertaining to him the said Mordecai his heirs and assigns forever as fully & amply to all intents purposes & Constructions whatsoever as the same was made Over to the said Richard Saltar by deeds of Sale from Dugle Mackolom bearing date the fifteenth day of July Anno Q D Domini 1719 and not otherwise Jn Witness whereof J have hereunto Sett

my Hand and Seale this Twenty sixth day of
May Anno Q. Domini 1726.

Richard Saltar (L. S.)

Sealed & Delivered
in the Presence of
　　　her
Geo X Morlat
　　　mark
Richard Saltar Jun
Ebenezer Saltar

April 5th 1727 Then appeared before John Anderson Esq[r] One of his Majestys Council for the
Province of New Jersey Richard Saltar Jun[r] who
being solemnly Sworn on the Holly Evangelists
of Almighty God did declare that he saw Richard Saltar above Named execute the same as his
Act and Deed. John Anderson Examined &
agrees with the original the word (Lincen*) in
the 11th line underlined was by mistake in Recording.

John Terrill Reg

In the year 1730 Mordecai Lincoln acquired of
Thomas Millard 303 acres of land (being a part of
the thousand acres granted to Andrew Robeson Feb-
ruary 20th, 1718, willed by him to his son Jonathan
Robeson, and granted by the last named to Thomas
Millard, October 27th, 1729).

The name of Mordecai Lincoln appears among
the Justices of the Peace under date of March 5,
1732-1733, and Dec. 3, 1733.

In 1735, Mordecai Lincoln's signature appears

---

* Cf. Record in Lib. 30 or D. 3, 130, Trenton, N. J.

WILL OF MORDECAI LINCOLN, OF EXETER, PA. (First Page.)

on the return of the reviewers of the road from
Schuylkill to Oley, as may be seen in the papers of
the Quarter Sessions of Philadelphia, 1735 and 1736.
It is clear from these documents that Mordecai
Lincoln migrated to Pennsylvania in or about the
year 1720, that he was an ironmonger and bought
land in that part of Pennsylvania where the iron
industry was developing and where it has continued
to flourish until the present day. He was thus following the tradition of his father who began the
iron industry in Massachusetts a generation before.

Mordecai Lincoln made his last will and testament February 22d, 1735. His signature was
affirmed and sworn to by two of the witnesses, Solomon Coles and John Bell, June 7th, 1736, at which
time the testator was evidently deceased. It is likely
that he died late in May, 1736, as the will naturally
would have been proven soon after the death of the
testator. His mortal remains were buried in the
Quaker burying ground, near Oley.* The text of
the Will runs thus:

> Jn the Name of God Amen J Mordecai Lincon
> of Amity in the County of philad^a in the province
> of pennsylv^a being sick and weak in body but of
> sound mind and Memory Do make this my last
> will and Testament in manner and form following
> revoking and hereby disanulling and making void
> all other and former Wills and Testaments by
> me made whether in word or Writing allowing
> this to be my last will and Testament and no other.

---

* The Exeter Meeting is evidently meant.

Jmprimis it is my mind that in ye first place my Just debts be honiestly paid.

Jtem J give and bequeath unto My son Mordecai Linkon the half of my land scituate in amity and to his heirs and assigns forever

Jtem J give and bequeath unto my son Thomas Linkon his heirs and assigns forever the one half of my Land in amity aforesaid.

With this proviso that if my present wife Mary should prove with Child at my Decease and bring forth a son, then J order that ye said Land be Divided into three equall parts, And that Mordecai shall have ye Lower most or South East part, and Thomas the Middle most and the posthumus ye uper part:

Jtem J give and bequeath unto my Daughters Hannah and Mary a Certain piece of Land at Matjaponix allread settled on them by a deed of gift.

Jtem J give unto my son John Lincon a Certain piece of Land Lying in the Jerseys Containing three hundred acres, and to his heirs and assigns forever.

Jtem J give and bequeath unto my Two daughters Anne & Sarah and to their heirs and assigns forever one hundred acres of Land lying at Matjaponix in the Jersey, which Land J do order my Executrix herein after Named to sell and divide ye money equally between them.

And J do hereby further order and appoint that if any one or more of my Children above named should happen to dye before they arrive to their full age then such share or shares of y^e

to be at her Disposall, and Liberty to remain on my plantation
at [....] Amity untill those my Children are at their Severall
ages, the better to enable my Wife to bring up all my Children
without wasting or embezelling what I have left them —

And I do likely nominate and appoint my Wife Mary Lincoln
my Whole and Sole Executrix of this my last Will and testament
And my Loving Friends and Neighbours Jonathan Roberson
[....] this my Will and Testament [....] truely performed
according to the true Intent and Meaning thereof —

The within named Mordecai Lincoln did Sign publish
[....] and declare that this present writing was his last
Will and Testament ye 22 day of february A.o Dom 1735
In the presence of us

Israel Robeson
[....]
John Bell [....]   Mordecai Lincoln

Philad. June [..] 1736 [....] personally appeared [....]
[....] and John Bell two of the [....] to the foregoing Will & the s.d
John Bell on his Oath, did severally declare they saw & heard Mordecai
Lincoln Sign [....] and declare the same Will to be his
Last Will & Testament and that at his doing thereof he was of sound
mind Memory and understanding to the best of their knowledge —

[....]

WILL OF MORDECAI LINCOLN, OF EXETER, PA. (Second Page.)
(Original in the City Hall, Philadelphia.)

A true Inventory of all and Singular y Goods Chattles and Credits of Mordecai Lincon Gent Deceaf praifed at Amity y 5th day of June A D 1736 by Ellis Hugh and Squire Boone

	£ s d
Imprimis To purfe and apparrel	10=00=00
To His books	02=00=00
To a bed £2:10f // a Cheft of drawers £1:10f	04=00=00
To an oval Table	00=15=00
To one bed £2: and a cheft of	02=06=00
To a Cheft and Looking Glafs	00=6=00
To Chaires and Pewter	2:4:0
To three guns and wooden ware	2:00=00
To Spinning Wheels and Iron potts	1:13=00
To Two beds and Earthen ware	2:12:00
To a Saddle one bed and a Trunk	2:00=00
To a Still and some Siverie	8=00=00
To Sheep	7=00=00
To Horned Cattle	30:00=00
To oxen	15=00=00
To a mare and Colt	2:00=00
To a Lamb and Gares	2:00=00
To a Small Cart, plow Harrow and gares	3=10=00
To Smith Tools	2:10=00
To an Iron Kittle	00=15=00
Carpenters Tools 10f Hares and axes 10f	1=00=00
To Negro Will	20=00=00
To Negro John for Seven years	10=00=00
praifed by us y Subfcribers y day and	£131:11=0

year Above written

Ellis Hugh

Squire Boone

deceased shall be Equally Divided amongst y^e surviving Children.

Jtem J give and bequeath unto my beloved Wife Mary all y^e residue or remainder of My Estate goods Chattles Quick & dead To be at her disposall, and Liberty to remain on My plantati[on] at Melar [?] Amity untill those my Children are at their severall ages, the better to enable my Wife to bring up all my Children without wasting or embezeling what I have left them.

And J do hereby nominate and appoint my Wife Mary Lincon my whole and sole Executrix of this my last Will and testam[ent.]

And my loving friends and Neighbours Jonathan Robeson and George Boone Trustees to assist my Executrix in & seeing this my Will and Testament well and truely perform [ed] according to ye true Intent and Meaning thereof.

The within named Mordecai Lincon did sign publish pronounce and declare that this present writing was his last will and Testament ye 22 day of ffebruary A° Dom¹ 1735

Jn the presence of us   Mordecai Lincon
Jsrael Robeson
Solomon Coles   aff 7th June 1736
John Bell   Iur eod

Philad^a June 7th 1736. Then personally appeard Solomon Coles and John Bell two of the witnesses to the foregoing Will & the sd Solomon on his solemn affirmation & the sd John Bell on his Oath did severally declare they saw & heard Mordecai Lincoln Sign Seal publish and declare the same Will to be his Last Will & Testament and that at the doing thereof he was of sound mind Memory and understanding to the best of their knowledge.

Coram Pet Evans Rec Gen

The widow of Mordecai Lincoln transfered her power of attorney January 17, 1742, to her son-in-law, William Tallman, of Amity Township. This is the instrument:

Know all Men by these presents that Mary Rodgers of Exeter in the County of Philad[a] in the Province of Pensylvania whole and Sole Executrix of Mordecai Lincon my deceased Husband (by Virtue of his last Will and Testament were Jmpowered to make Sale certain Lands as by the said Will will at Large Appear) Know ye that I the said Mary Rodgers for divers Good causes and considerations me thereunto moving Have placed made Ordained Constituted & appointed, and in my stead and place have put and Authorized my son in Law William Tallman of Amity in the County aforesaid, yeoman, my True and Layfull Attorney for me and in my Name and to my use and Behoof, to Enter into all these Lands Containing One hundred Acres lying on Matjaponix in East Jersey with all their Rights members and appurtenances thereunto belonging to Enter all and every part & parcel thereof for me and in my Name to Survey and for me and in my name to bargain Sell Lease or grant to such person or persons & for such Estate for Life Inheritance or

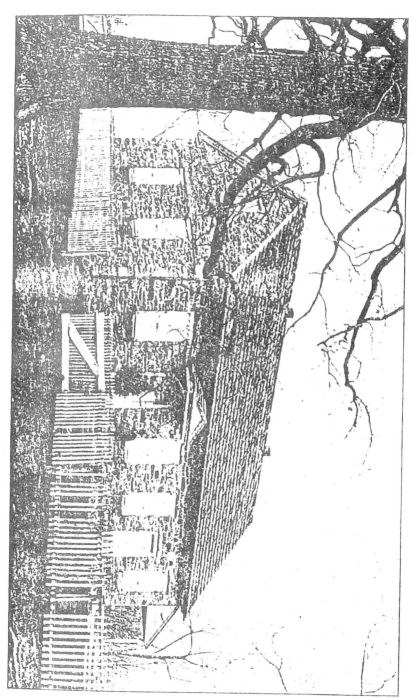

FRIENDS' MEETING HOUSE, EXETER, BERKS COUNTY.

Otherwise & for Such Sum or Sumes of money
as by my said Attourney shall be though[t] meet
and requisite to the utermost & best comodity and
profit of me, and deed and deeds of the same
grants and Estates so to be made for me and in
my Name to Seal and as my deed to deliver unto
the parties to whome the same shall be so made,
And Acquittances & other Discharges for me and
in my Name to seal and deliver Hereby giving
and granted unto my said Attourney my whole &
full power and Authority in touching and concerning the premisses to do—Execute proceed and fin-
ish in all things in as Large and Ample manner
and form as J myself might or Ought to do if J
were personally present, And Ratifying & allow-
ing whatsoever my said Attorney shall Lawfully
Act and do according to the True Jntent & meaning
of these presents, Jn Witness whereof J have hereunto set my hand & Seal the 17th day of January
A⁰. D⁰. 1742.

Mary Rogers (ss)

Sealed and delivered
in the presence of us

Geo : Boone—Roger Rogers

Be it Remembered that On the 17th day of January 1742. before me George Boone Esqʳ One of
his Majesties Justices of the peace for the City
& County of Philadᵃ came Mary Rodgers and
acknowledged the within power of Attourney to
be her deed—Witness my hand yᵉ day of Year
above written.

Geo : Boone (ss)

CHAPTER III.

ABRAHAM LINCOLN IN PENNSYLVANIA.

Abraham Lincoln, the brother of Mordecai, also migrated to Pennsylvania and settled in Springfield Township, Chester County, in or about the year 1729, and died there in 1745. He was a blacksmith as well as a yeoman. The following records, referring to him, have been found in the documents still extant.

Abraham Lincoln or "Lincon" is mentioned as one of the 22 Jurors in the General Quarter Sessions of the Peace, of Monmouth County, New Jersey, Nov. 22, 1720. With Robert Lawrence and Corneles van Horen he made an inventory of Peter Gordon's personal estate May 13, 1725.*

The first appearance of Abraham Lincoln's name in Pennsylvania is found in a deed issued by Thomas Williams, of Freehold, New Jersey, to "Abraham Lincon of Springfield, in the County of Chester and province of Pennsylvania" under date of January 16, 1729. From this document we learn that Abraham Lincoln by a "bargain of Sale" for one year had already occupied the tract in question which was situated on Crum Creek. It would thus appear that Abraham Lincoln moved to Pennsylvania in January or March, 1728, as we may suppose his occupancy followed quickly upon the "bargain of

---

* Cf. *New Jersey Archives*, First Series xxiii, p. 190.

Sale" which seems to have been dated January 15th, 1728. The deed, recorded in West Chester, Pa., runs as follows:

"THIS INDENTURE made the Sixteenth day of Ianuary in the Year of our Lord one Thousand and Seven hundred and Twenty nine (thirty) Between Thomas Williams of freehold in the County of Monmouth and Prov^e of New Jersey Yeoman of the one part and Abraham Lincon of Springfield in the County of Chester and province of Pennsylvania Yeoman of the other part WITNESSETH that the said Thomas Williams for an in Consideration of the sum of Three hundred and Twenty pounds Lawful money of America to him in hand paid by the s^d Abraham Lincon the receipt whereof is hereby acknowledged and thereof doth acquit & forever Discharge the said Abraham Lincon his heirs and assigns by these presents Have Granted bargained sold aliened enfeoffed released & Confirmed and by these presents do grant bargain sell alien enfeoffe release and Confirm unto the said Abraham Lincon his heirs & assigns all that Tract of Land Situate in Springfield aforesaid Containing three hundred acres withe allowances of Ten acres on the hundred all the Messuage or Tenement & Plantation thereon BEGINNING at a White Oak standing by Crum Creek thence north fifty five degrees Easterly by Bartho[l]omew Coppocks land three hundred and sixty seven perches to a Post thence south Thirty five degrees Easterly by Thomas Taylors land one hundred and Twenty eight perches to a Black Oak thence south fifty-five degrees West by George

Lowns Land four hundred and Twenty Seven
perches to Crum Creek thence along the said Creek
on the Several Courses thereof To the place of Beginning Containing three hundred and Thirty acres
TOGETHER with all the Houses out Houses Edifices Buildings Gardens orchards mines minerals
Wods undwoods Medws [sic] Marshes Swamps
criples ways waters waterCourses fishings fowlings
haukings Huntings Rights Libertys Priviledges Improvements hereditaments & apurtenances whatsoever thereunto belonging or in any wise appertaining of all which said Land and premises hereby
Granted with their appurtenances the said Abraham Lincon is now in actual Possession by force
and Virtue of a bargain and Sale to him thereof
made by the said Thomas Williams for the Term
of one Year as by an Indenture in that behalf
made bearing Date the day next before the day
of the date hereof may apear and the Reversions
and remainders rents Issues and profits thereof
and all Deeds Writings and Evidences whatsoever
Concerning the same To HAVE & to HOLD the said
Messuage or Tenement Plantation and three hundred and Thirty acres of land and premises hereby
Granted or mentioned so to be with their Appurtenances unto the said Abraham Lincon and his
heirs to the only proper use and behoof of the
said Abraham Lincon his heirs and assigns forever UNDER the Yearly Quitrent hereafter accruing to the Lord of the fee thereof AND the said
Thomas Williams & his heirs the s^d Messuage or
Tenement three hundred and Thirty acres of Land

Hereditaments and premises hereby Granted with their Appurtenances unto the said Abraham Lincon his heirs and Assigns against· him the said Thomas Williams, and his heirs & against him the said Thomas Williams [any] persons whomsoever Lawfully Claiming or to Claime by from or under him or his heirs shall and will Warant and Defend forever by these presents AND the said Thomas Williams for himself and his heirs doth Covenant Promise and Grant to and with the said Abraham Lincon his heirs & assigns by these presents Thatt he hath in himself Good rightfull Lawful and Absolute Power and Authority to Grant bargain sell & Convey all the said Messuage or Tenement Plantation land & premises hereby Granted with their Appurtenances unto the said Abraham Lincon his heirs and assigns in manner aforesaid AND thatt the said Abraham Lincon his heirs and assigns shall or Lawfully may from time to time and at all times hereafter forever freely quietly & peaceably have hold Occupy Possess and Enjoy the sᵈ Mesuage Plantation Land and premises and every part thereof with the Appurtenances & receive and Take all the rents Issues and profits thereof without any manner of Lett Suit Trouble or Molestation whatsoever by any person or persons whomsoever AND ALSO that the said Mesuage land and premises with their appurtenances now are and from time to time forever hereafter shall remain Continue and be unto the said Abraham Lincon [and] his heirs free and Clear and freely and clearly aquited and discharged of & from all

and all manner of former & other bargains Sales
Gifts Grants Jointures Devises Mortgages Intails
Rents Arrearages of Rents [?] little charges or Incumbrances whatsoever the proprietors Quitrents
hereafter acrueing for the same only Excepted AND
LASTLY that he the said Thomas and his heirs and
assigns and all and every other person & persons
Whomsoever Lawfully Claiming or to Claim the
said Messuage Land and premises hereby Granted
shall and will from time to time and at all times
hereafter upon the request Cost and Charge in the
Law of the said Abraham Lincon his heirs or assigns make do Execute and Acknowledge or Cause
so to be all & every such further and other reasonable act & acts Deed or Deeds Device or Devices
in the Law for the further and better assuring and
Confirmation of the said Messuage Land & Plantation hereby Granted with their appurtenances
unto the said Abraham Lincon his heirs and assigns as by him or them or by his or their Counsel
Learned in the Law shall be reasonably Devised
advised or Requred [sic]

     IN WITNESS whereof the said Thomas Williams
hath hereunto set his hand and affixed his Seal the
day & Year first abov Written.

                 Thomas Williams   (Seal)

     Sealed and Delivered
by the said Thomas
Williams in the pres-
ence of

Robert Lawrence
John Coward—

BE IT REMEMBERED the fourteenth day of September 1747 Before me Benjamin Shoemaker Esqʳ one of the justices &c personally Came and appeared William Lawrence of the City of Philadelphia Merchant and the within Written Indenture subscribed Thomas (X) Williams to Seal & with the names Robᵗ Lawrence & John Coward &c."

[W. Lawrence attested the signature of his father Robert and the deed was recorded Aug. 22, 1785.]

This same year, 1729, and later, we find the name of Abraham Lincoln among the taxables of Chester County, as the following excerpts from the originals show:

1729 Springfield
Abraham Lincon ....14 s. d.
1730 Springfield
Abraham Lincon....................12 s. d.

The name Abraham Lincoln continues to be written this way until 1739, when we have the following entry:

1739 Springfield
Abraham Linghorn ....
1740 Springfield
Abram Lincoln

Abraham Lincoln, of Springfield, before migrating from New Jersey, owned two considerable tracts of land in Monmouth County, New Jersey, as may be seen from the land records. One of these tracts,

containing 240 acres, was granted to him by Safety
Borden, February 11th, 1722, and the other tract,
containing 200 acres, was granted him by Abraham
Vanhorn, March 25th, 1725. After purchasing the
tract in Springfield Township, on Crum Creek, from
Thomas Williams, Lincoln sold both of the above
tracts in East Jersey to Thomas Williams, April 29,
1730, for the sum of 590 pounds. The following
deed relates the brief title and sets forth the conditions of sale:

THIS INDENTURE, Made the Twenty ninth day
of April in the third Year of the Reign of Our
Sovereign Lord George the Second by the Grace
of God of Great Britain France & Ireland King,
Defender of the Faith &c. Anno Domini One
Thousand Seven hundred & thirty Between Abraham Lincon of the County of Monmouth in the
Eastern Division of the Province of New Jersey
Blacksmith of the one part And Thomas Wil-
liams of the Same County Yeoman of the other
part WITNESSETH that the said Abraham Lincon
for & in Consideration of the Sum of Five Hun-
dred & Ninety Pounds Current Money of the Said
Province to him in hand Paid before the Enseal-
ing & Delivery of these Presents by him the said
Thomas Williams the Receit whereof he the Said
Abraham Lincon doth hereby acknowledge & him-
self to be therewith fully & Entirely Satisfied
Contented & Paid & thereof & of & from every
Part & parcel thereof Doth fully clearly & absolutely Acquit Exonerate & Discharge him the
Said Thomas Williams his Heirs Executors Ad-

ministrators & Every of them forEver by these
presents HATH granted bargained & Sold Aliened
enfeoffed & Confirmed And by these Presents
Doth fully clearly & absolutely Grant Bargain
& Sell Alien enfeoffe Release Convey & Confirm unto him the Said Thomas Williams his
Heirs & Assigns forEver All those two Tracts
of Land Scituate Lying & Being near Cross-
weeks in the County aforesaid herein after Abut-
ted Bounded & Described Viz: All that Tract of
Land which was Granted & Confirmed unto him
the Said Abraham Lincon by deed from Safety
Borden bearing date the Eleventh day of February Anno Domini 1722 Containing Two Hundred
& forty Acres be the Same more or less BEGIN-
NING at a Stake Standing in the Clear Land, which
is a corner of Benjamin Bordens Land Twenty
five Chains from Burlington Path & Ten Chains
Eastward of the Land in possession of Richard
Borden & Running North North West Twenty
three Chains Sixty five Links to the South East
Corner of Abraham Vanhorns Land And from
said Beginning Stake Running North Seventy
Seven Degrees Easterly Forty & two Chains, Then
South East to Burlington Path & North Easterly
along the Path to the Pines & following the Pines
to the corner of John Limings Land Then South
Seventy Seven Degrees West along said Limmings
line to the above named Vanhornes land and
following said Vanhornes lines to the South
East Corner of his Land as above mentioned
BOUNDED North Westwardly by Vanhorns &
Limmings Land South Westwardly by Benja-

min Bordens Land South Eastwardly partly by
Benjamin Borden & partly by Burlington Path
North Eastwardly by the Pines AND ALSO All that
tract of Land which was granted & Confirmed
to him the Said Abraham Lincon by Deed from
Abraham Vanhorn bearing Date the Twenty fifth
day of March Anno Domini 1725 Containing Two
Hundred Acres—BEGINNING at a stake Standing
in the rere of the Lott of Land formerly Job
Throckmortons of which Lott this Two Hundred
Acres is part, which Stake Stands Ten Chains
from the South Westernmost Corner of the Said
Lott & from thence running South South East
Fifty One Chains & thirty five Links Thence North
Seventy Seven Degrees Easterly Thirty One
Chains & twenty Links to the Line of Land lately
Sold to James Borden, Thence North North West
Eleven Chains & an half to a Maple Tree
by a Brook marked on four sides Thence up the
said Brook Ten Chains & forty Links to where the
Line of the said Land sold to James Borden cross-
es said Brook Thence North North West Thirty
seven Chains & one Rodd Thence South seventy
seven Degrees Westwardly Forty two Chains to
the Place where it Began Bounded Southerly Ten
Chain short of the Land on which Richard Borden formerly lived, Easterly by the first above-
mentioned Tract of Land Northerly by the Land
Sold to James Borden Westerly by the Rere Line
of said Lott Together with all & all manner of
Housings Buildings Edifices Structures Barns
Stables Orchards Fencings Feedings Improvements Pastures Meadows Woods Trees Waters

Brooks Springs Ponds Pools Pits Easements Profits Commodities Royalties Liberties Advantages Emoluments Hereditaments & Appurtenances whatsoever To the said Two Tracts of Land Belonging or in any manner of Ways thereunto Appertaining And also all the Estate Right Title Interest Possession Property Claims & Demand whatsoever of him the said Abraham Lincon & his Heirs as well in Law as in Equity of in or unto the said Two Tracts & Granted & Bargained Premises with the Appurtenancies with the Reversion & Reversions Remainder & Remainders thereof & of every part & parcel thereof as fully & amply to all Intents Constructions & Purposes whatsoever as the same was Granted & Confirmed unto him the said Abraham Lincon in & by the two Deeds before mentioned Relation to the Same being had more fully & at large may Appear To Have and to Hold the said Two Tracts of Land & Granted & Bargained Premises with all & singular the Rights Members & Appurtenances to the same belonging unto him the said Thomas Williams his Heirs & Assigns for Ever To the only proper Use Benefit & behoof of him the said Thomas Williams his Heirs & Assigns for Ever Yeilding & Paying therefore Yearly and Every Year hereafter unto the said Abraham Lincon his Heirs & Assigns for Ever as an Acknowledgment for the first mentioned Tract of Land upon the Feast of St. Michael the Arch-Angel the Sum of One Penny good & Lawful Money, when the same shall be legally Demanded upon the Premises And he the said Abraham Lincon for himself his Heirs Executors & Administrators Doth Covenant Promise Grant & Agree to and with him the said Thomas Williams his Heirs & Assigns by these presents in manner & form following Viz^t: That at the time of the Sealing & Delivery hereof he the said Abraham Lincon is Lawfully Seized of the Said Two Tracts of Land as above bounded & all & singular & every the Premises & Appurtenances thereof of a good, sure, pure, perfect & absolute Lawful Indefeazable Estate of Inheritance in the Law, in his proper Demesne as of Fee without any Condition or Limitation of any Use or Uses Estate or Estates in or to any person or persons whatsoever so as to Alter Change Charge Defeat Determine or make Void the Same, or any part thereof And that he the Said Abraham Lincon hath in himself good Rightfull Power and absolute Lawful Authority to Grant Bargain & Sell the same & Every part thereof unto him the Said Thomas Williams his Heirs & Assigns for ever in manner aforesaid And that the same now is free & from time to time & at all times hereafter Shall remain & be free & clear to him the Said Thomas Williams, his Heirs & Assigns for Ever from all & all manner of former & other Gifts Grants Bargains Sales Leases Mortgages & of & from all other Titles Troubles Charges Demands & Incumbrances whatsoever had made Committed done or suffered to bedone by him the Said Abraham Lincon or any other Person or Persons whatsoever by from or under him so as to Alter Change Charge Defecit or make Void this Same.

His Rents or Services that for the last mentioned Tract Shall become due to the Lords Proprietors only Excepted AND FURTHER he the Said Abraham Lincon for him-self his Heirs Executors & Administrators Doth hereby Covenant Promise Grant & Agree the Said Two Tracts of Land & Granted & Bargained Premises with the Appurtenances unto him the Said Thomas Williams & his Heirs & Assigns, against him the Said Abraham Lincon & his Heirs & all & Every other Person or Persons whatsoever lawfully laying claim to the same or to any part or parcel thereof shall & will Warrant & for Ever by these Presents Defend In Witness whereof he the Said Abraham Lincon hath hereunto Set his hand & Seal the day and year first above written

Abraham (L. S.) Lincon

The written within Instrument
Sealed & Delivered in the presence of
Benj. Price Law^r Smyth

An old document, the petition of Mordecai Taylor of the township of Springfield for a tavern license, contains the signature of Abraham Lincoln. This petition sets forth so vividly the primitive conditions of the Great Road leading from Darby to Springfield in 1743, that it is printed here:

Chester Co. To his Majesties Justices of the peace at the Court of General Quarter Sessions held at Chester the 31st day of August Annoq Domini 1743—
The Petition of Mordecai Taylor of the Township of Springfield—
Humbly Sheweth

That whereas your Petitioner living on the Great Road leading from Darby to Springfield & so into Conostogoe Road being a Commodious place for a House of Entertainment and no Tavern being within four Miles of him, And Travellers daily travelling that Road And People going back and forward sometimes Twenty or Thirty Waggons of a Day And Calling at your Petitioners House, which is a great Trouble & Expense to Yo^r Petit^r Therefore he prays that your Honours would be pleased to grant him a Recommendation to the Governor for a Lycence Accordingly And your Petit^r as in duty bound shall ever pray

Mordecai Taylor.

We whose names are hereunto subscribed being well Acquainted with the above Petitioner believe him to be a suitable person to keep a Public house of Entertainment And prays that You would be pleased to grant him a Recommendation to the Governor for a Lycence Accordingly

B Davis	Joseph Powell Jos: Levis
Thomas Taylor	Bartholomew Coppock
John Owen	Mordecai Massey
Jno Levis	James Rhoades
Abr^m Lincon	John Rhoads
M Maddock	Thomas Fall
James Crozer	Joseph Maris
Jno Gibbons	Bernhard Van Leer
Jos. Harvey	Jsaac Collier *

* From the collection of Mr. Gilbert Cope, who kindly furnished the writer with a photograph of the Petition.

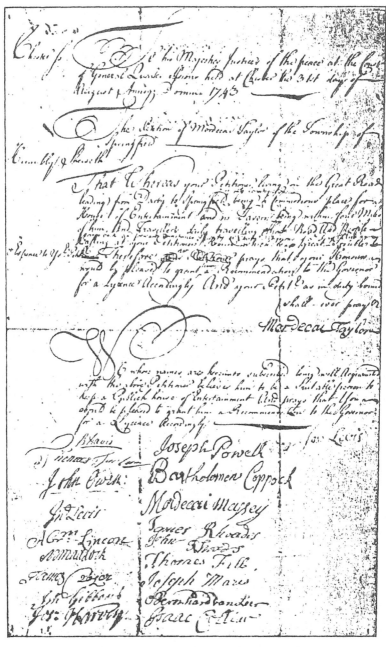

PETITION FOR TAVERN LICENSE, SHOWING SIGNATURE OF ABRAHAM
LINCOLN, OF SPRINGFIELD.

(Original in the Possession of Mr. Gilbert Cope.)

In the year 1744 Abraham Lincoln, of Springfield, bought property in Elbow lane in the city of Philadelphia, from William Clare and from John Clare and John Clare's sister, Esther. In his will Lincoln mentions a property bought of Humphrey Clase (Classe) in the same city. In the deeds to the Clare properties, Lincoln is spoken of as "Yeoman of Springfield, Chester County." The relation of Humphrey Clase in the transaction appears in the deeds which follow. The deed of William Clare conveying this portion of the tract in question and received from the estate of his father (William Clare, deceased), here follows in its essential parts:

THIS INDENTURE Made the Twenty Ninth day of March in the year of our Lord one thousand seven hundred and forty four Between William Clare of the City of Philadelphia in the Province of Pennsylvania Cordwainer of the one part and Abraham Lincon of Springfield in the County of Chester Yeoman of the other part Whereas in and by certain Indentures of lease and release bearing date respectively the twenty third and twenty fourth days of June 1720 made between Joshua Carpenter of the said City Gentleman and Elizabeth his wife of the one part and John Rakestraw of the same City Carter and Ruth his wife of the other part he the said Joshua Carpenter and Elizabeth his wife did for the considerations therein mentioned grant release and confirm unto the said Iohn Rakestraw and Ruth his wife A Certain piece or parcel of ground situate lying and being in Philadelphia aforesaid Containing in front or breadth on Elbow Lane thirty seven feet and in length forty four feet Bounded northward with Elbow Lane aforesaid Eastward with George Emlen's lot Southward by the back of Chesnut Street lots and westward with other ground of the said Joshua Carpenter with its appurtenances to hold to them the said Iohn Rakestraw and Ruth his wife their heirs and assigns forever Yielding and Paying yearly and every year unto the said Ioshua Carpenter his heirs and assigns the rent or sum of two pounds nine shillings and four pence lawful money of America at the rates appointed by the late Act of Parliament for ascertaining the rates of foreign coin in the Plantations of America * * [recital of earlier title] * * * * * * * *

Now this indenture witnesseth that for and in consideration of the sum of fifty pounds lawful money of the Province aforesaid unto the said William Clare party thereto well and truly paid by the said Abraham Lincon at or before the sealing and delivery of these presents the receipt whereof is hereby acknowledged and thereof doth acquit and forever discharge the said Abraham Lincon his heirs executors and administrators forever he the said William Clare party hereto Hath granted bargained sold released and confirmed and by these presents Doth grant bargain sell release and confirm unto the said Abraham Lincon in his actual possession now being, and unto his heirs and assigns All that the said westernmost tenement new erected on the said piece of ground before described on the south side of Elbow Lane

Containing thirty seven feet by forty four with a proportionate part of the said piece of ground thereunto belonging * * * * * * * * *

IN WITNESS whereof the said parties to these presents have hereunto interchangeably set their hands and seals the day and year first above written

William Clare (Seal)

Sealed and Delivered
in the Presence of us

Harry Travers Ioseph Breintnall

[Signature of Grantor acknowledged March 30 1744. Recorded April 29 1835]

The deed* of John Clare and Humphrey Clase (the husband of John Clare's sister Esther) conveying the shares of John and Esther to Abraham Lincoln explains the appearance of Humphrey Clase in the transaction, and shows that Abraham Lincoln, of Springfield, bought at least three of the four shares of the tract of ground left by William Clare, Sr., to his four children, George, William, Jr., John and Esther (who married Humphrey Clase):

THIS INDENTURE Made the nineteenth day of November in the year of our Lord one thousand seven hundred and forty four Between John Clare of the City of Philadelphia Cordwainer and Abigal his wife and Humphrey Classe of the said City

---

* Deed Book 60, p. 601 ff, City Hall, Philadelphia.

Mariner and Esther his wife (sister of the said Iohn Clare) of the one part and Abraham Lincon of Springfield in the County of Chester Yeoman of the other part Whereas in and by a certain Indenture of lease and release bearing date the twenty third and twenty fourth days of Iune one thousand seven hundred and twenty made between Ioshua Carpenter of the said City Gentleman and Elizabeth his wife of the one part and Iohn Rakestraw of the said City Carter and Ruth his wife of the other part he the said Ioshua Carpenter and Elizabeth his wife for and in the Consideration therein mentioned did grant release and Confirm unto the said Iohn Rakestraw and Ruth his wife A Certain piece or parcel of land situate lying and being in Philadelphia aforesaid Containing in breadth upon Elbow Lane thirty seven feet and in length forty four feet Bounded northward with Elbow Lane aforesaid eastward with George Emlen's lot southward with the back of Chestnut Street lots and westward with the other ground of the said Ioshua Carpenter with the appurtenances to hold to them the said Ioshua Rakestraw and Ruth his wife their heirs and assigns forever Yielding and paying yearly and every year unto the said Ioshua Carpenter his heirs and assigns the rent or sum of two pounds nine shillings and four pence lawful money of America at the rate appointed by the late act of Parliament for ascertaining the rates of foreign coins in the Plantations in America on the twenty

fourth day of Iune yearly forever with clauses of
reentry and distress for non payment AND WHERE-
AS in and by a certain Indenture bearing date the
first day of July 1721 (And Recorded at Philadelphia in Deed Book vol 2 page 204 &c) made
between the said Iohn Rakestraw and Ruth his
wife of one part and William Clare of the said
City Cordwainer father of the said Iohn Clare of
the other part they the said Iohn Rakestraw and
Ruth his wife for the consideration therein mentioned did grant release and confirm unto the said
William Clare his heirs and assigns all that the
above mentioned and described piece or parcel of
land with a certain messuage or tenement there on
built and erected by the said Iohn Rakestraw Together also with all and singular other the buildings improvements ways alleys passages waters
water courses rights easements rights liberties
privileges hereditaments and appurtenances whatsoever thereunto belonging and the reversions and
remainders rents issues and profits thereof and
all the estate right title interest use possession
property claim and demand of them the said Iohn
Rakestraw and Ruth his wife of in and to the
hereby granted premises and true copies of all
deeds evidences and writings concerning the premises to be had and taken at the proper costs and
charges of the said William Clare his heirs or
assigns which last recited Indenture contains a
covenant on the part of the said William Clare his
heirs and assigns well and truly to pay and discharge yearly forever the said rent of two pounds

nine shillings and four pence AND WHEREAS the
said William Clare after having built and erected
another messuage or tenement on the said described lot of ground made his last will and testament bearing date the seventeenth day of the
fourth month one thousand seven hundred and
thirty two wherein he disposed of his estate in the
world viz. I give and bequeath unto my beloved
wife Esther Clare all my real and personal estate
goods and chattels whatsoever to have the full
and free use of them during her life and after her
decease to be divided equally amongst all my children Item I make my aforesaid wife full and
sole executrix of this my last will and testament
And Whereas the said Executrix survived the said
testator some time and is since deceased and there
upon the children namely George Clare William
Clare Iohn Clare and Esther Clare by Indenture
bearing date the Sixteenth day of October 1742
and then intended to be recorded [Recorded in
Book 9 Vol. 5 page 101 &c] and an amicable par-
tition and division of the said Estate whereby it
was agreed among other things that the said Iohn
Clare and his said sister Esther shall hold enjoy
and have the Easternmost which is the largest of
the two tenements erected on the said piece of
ground of thirty seven feet in breadth by forty
four feet in length with a proportionable part of
the same piece of ground Together with the appurtenances which Easternmost Tenement and the
ground thereto belonging are bargained and sold
and intended to be hereby conveyed unto the said

Abraham Lincon his heirs and assigns. Now this indenture witnesseth that the said Iohn Clare and Abigail his wife and Humphrey Clase and Esther his wife for and in consideration of the sum of one hundred and twenty pounds lawful money of Pennsylvania to them in hand paid and secured to be paid the receipt whereof is hereby acknowledged HAVE and each of them hath granted bargained sold released and confirmed and by these presents Do and each of them DOTH grant bargain sell release and confirm unto the said Abraham Lincon and to his heirs and assigns ALL that the said Easternmost tenement and the ground thereunto belonging situate on the South side of Elbow Lane as aforesaid Together with all the ways alleys waters water courses rights [?] easements rights liberties privileges hereditaments and appurtenances thereunto belonging or in any wise appurtaining and all the estate right title interest use possession property claim and demands of them the said grantors or either or any of them of in or to the hereby granted premises and true copies of all deeds evidences and writings concerning the same to have and to hold the said Easternmost tenement situate on the south side of Elbow Lane and a proportionable part thereto belonging of the said lot of ground of thirty seven foot by forty four foot hereditaments and premises hereby granted or mentioned or inteded to be granted with the appurtenances unto the said Abraham Lincon and his heirs to the use and behoof of the said Abraham Lincon his heirs and assigns forever

Subject to a proportionable part of the said recited
rent of two pounds nine shillings and four pence
And the said Iohn Clare and Abigail his wife and
Humphey Clase and Esther his wife the hereby
granted premises against them and each of them
and all persons lawfully claiming under them unto
the said Abraham Lincon his heirs and assigns
shall and will warrant and forever defend by these
presents And the said Iohn Clare for himself his
heirs executors and administrators and for the
said Abigail his wife and the said Humphey Clase
for himself his heirs executors and administrators for the said Esther his wife do respectively
covenant promise and grant that they the said Iohn
Clare and Abigail his wife and Humphey Clase and
Esther his wife shall and will at any time or
times hereafter at the reasonable request cost and
charges in the law of the said Abraham Lincon his
heirs or assigns make execute and acknowledge
or cause so to be all and every such further and
other reasonable act and acts deed or deeds device
or devices in law for the further and better assur-
ance and confirmation of the said tenement and
proportionable piece of ground hereditaments and
premises hereby granted as mentioned to be granted with the appurtenances unto the said Abraham
Lincon his heirs and assigns (under the proportionable part of rent aforesaid) as by him or them
or his or their counsel learned in the law shall be
reasonably devised advised or required In Witness whereof the said parties to these presents have

hereunto interchangeably set their hands and seals
the day and year first above written

Esther Classe	(Seal)
Humphrey Classe	(Seal)
Iohn Clare	(Seal)
Abigail Clare	(Seal)

Sealed and Delivered in
    the Presence of us
Jos Howell   Joseph Brentnall

The Twentieth day of November 1744

Before me Joshua Maddox Esquire one of the
Iustices &c came the within named Iohn Clare and
Abigail his wife and Humphey Classe and Esther
his wife and acknowledged the with in written
Indenture to be their and each of their act and
deed and desired the same may be recorded And
the said Abigail and Esther being of full age and
apart examined willingly consented.

Witness my Hand and seal the day and year
aforesaid

Recorded April 29th 1835

Josh. Maddox   (Seal)

Abraham Lincoln made his will April 15, 1745.
He died a very few days later, for the inventory is
dated April 30, 1745. Both the will and the inventory are interesting documents and shed much light
upon the history of this branch of the family. Abraham bequeathed his estate as follows:

J ABRAHAM LINCON of Springfield in the County
of Chester in the Province of Pensilvania Blacksmith being sick and weak in body but of well dis-
posing mind and Memory Praise be given to Almighty God therefore but in Consideration of the
Uncertainty of this Mortal state and not knowing
how it may please the Lord to deal with me at
this time DO make and Ordain this my last Will
and Testament in Manner and form following
First and Principally I recommend my Soul into
the hands of God that gave it and my body I com-
mit to the Earth to be buried in a Christian like
and decent manner at the discretion of my Executors AND as Touching such worldly Estate as it
hath pleased the Lord to bestow upon me I give
and dispose thereof as followeth IMPRIMIS my
will is that in the first place all my Just debts and
funeral Expenses be duly paid and discharged
ITEM I give to my son Iohn all and singular the
Land and Premises with the Appurtenances / it
being part and parcel of the Plantation whereon
I now dwell / Lying on the North East side of the
Road leading to Chester to HOLD to him my said
son Iohn his Heirs and Assigns for ever but if my
son Iohn should happen to dye before he Attains
to the age of Twenty one Years then my will is
and I give all the said Land unto my son Abraham
his Heirs and Assigns forever ITEM I give and devise unto my son Iacob all the Residue of this my
Plantation Situate on the South West side the
Road aforsaid with all and Singular the Appurtenances to Hold to him my said son Iacob his
Heirs and Assigns for ever PROVIDED also and
Upon Condition Nevertheless that my son Iacob

THE WILL OF ABRAHAM LINCOLN, OF SPRINGFIELD.
(Original in City Hall, Philadelphia.)

Builds a Brick dwelling House for the Use of my son Iohn at some Convenient place on the land devised to my son Iohn as aforsaid at some time within the Term of Ten Years after the date of this my Will which House shall be Seventeen foot Square from out to out Cellar'd Under and Carried Up two story high with a Cedar Roof and Windows Suitable to the Building ITEM I give and devise Unto my son Mordecai if he Returns into this Province within the Term of Seven Years Next after my decease all that Messuage or Tenement which I purchased of William Clayer Situate in the City of Philadelphia TO HOLD to him my said son Mordecai his Heirs and Assigns forever but if it should so happen that my son Mordecai shall not Return before the expiration of the Term aforsaid then my will is and I do give the said Messuage or Tenement Unto my son Isaac his Heirs and Assigns forever Provided Nevertheless that my son Isaac pay or cause to be paid Unto my son Mordecai if in Case he Returnes at any time after the Seven Years aforsaid the sum of ffive Pounds of Lawfull money of Pensilvania ITEM I give devise and bequeath Unto my daughter Rebecca my other Messuage or Tenement in the City of Philadelphia / Ioyning to the other before mentioned / which I Purchased of Humphry Clase and Iohn Clayor TO HOLD to her my said daughter Rebecca and to the Lawfull heirs of her body for ever but if she should happen to dye before the Age of Twenty one Years or without Issue then my will is and I give the said Messuage or Tenement Unto my son Isaac his Heirs and Assigns for ever ITEM I give Unto my daughter Sara my best feather bed with furniture as also the one half part of the Linnen Usually kept in my large chest ITEM I give Unto my son Abraham the sum of Thirty Six Pounds which I lent him some time since AND further my will is that all the Residue of my Estate after debts and Funeral Expenses paid as aforsaid and Sufficient for the Maintenance of my son John Untill he Arrives to the Age of Fourteen Years / as well Real as Personal whatsoever and wheresoever I give Unto my two sons / to witt / Abraham and Isaac to be divided in two Equal parts or portions share and share alike AND I Nominate Constitute and Appoint my two friends / to witt / Robert Taylor of Marple in the County of Chester aforsaid and Ioshua Thompson of Ridley in the County aforsaid Executors of this my last will and Testament AND I Revoke disanul and make void all and every other will and wills by me at any time heretofore made and do Ratifie & Confirm this and no other to be my Last Will and Testament IN WITNESS whereof I have hereunto sett my hand and seal this ffifteenth day of April in the Year of our Lord One Thousand Seven Hundred and fforty ffive.—   Abraham Lincon

Signed Sealed Published and delivered by Abraham Lincon the Testator to be his last will and Testament in the Presence of Us.

Emanuel Lownes   aff
John morton   Jur   24 April 1745
Jsa. Pearson affirm

A True Inventory of all and Singular the Goods Chattles Rights and Credits which were of Abraham Lincoln late of Springfield County of Chester Dec. as they were appraised by the Subscribers at the Request of Robert Taylor and Joshua Thomson Executors of the last will and testament of said Dec.

April the 16. 1745

	£	s	d
Purse and apparel	6	12	0
Bills and Bonds	68	0	0 ¼
One Negro Man	20	0	0
One Bed and furniture	16	16	0
Six Large Silver Spoons	6	0	0
One Clock £12. One Desk £4. One Case of Drawers £4.10	20	10	0
One Looking Glass £2.10 One Large table £1. One Case of bottles 14/6	4	4	0
Chairs £1. Walnut Chest £1.10. Square Table One little £2	3	18	0
Books 15/6. One Warming pan 15/6. One Iron 15/6. One pestle 7/6	2	12	6
Three Beds Bedding and Bedsteds	1	3	0
Pewter £ ... Glass & paper ware ...	6	16	0
One Brass Kettle & other brass and tin ware ...	3	11	0
Table linen Sheets and Bedlinen	12	3	0
Two Chests £1.10. One Box 5/6. Tables £1.4.0 ... Chairs 15	3	15	0
Four Iron Pots £1.14.6. Tea kettle, sauce pot & warming pan £1.10	4	16	0
Andirons Gridirons firetongs and tongs £1.10. ...	11	—	0
... Box Irons	1	4	11
Baskets ...	...	...	...
... horse ... £1	1	0	3
One Cross cut brush scaling iron five forks, fire coals and tongs	0	17	0
Hogsheads, Barrels, tubs tubs, Churn and cotton ware	1	16	0
Dry'd Beef and Bacon	1	14	2
Smiths Tools and Grind Stone	6	14	0
One Cart, plow, Harrows and Sundry Implements of Husbandry	8	1	3
One Horse £6.10. One Mare £9. One Colt £5.10	23	0	0
One Mare and Colt £1.10. One Old Horse 5/6	1	15	0
One Bull £1.15. Seven Cows £21. Two Oxen £8	30	15	0
Six Steers £12. Five Young Cattle £6.5. Three Calves £1.10	19	15	0
Seventeen Sheep & Eight Lambs £7.10. Four Hogs £1.10	9	0	0
Wheat 95 buf. at 2/6. Oats 23 buf. at 1/3	13	15	10
16¾ Acres of Wheat and Rye at 14/ p acre	11	0	10 ¼
3¾ Acres of Oats at 5/ p acre	0	11	6 ¼
Lumber	0	1	0
	329	16	10

Appraised by us:

John ...

John Hall

CHAPTER IV.

CHILDREN OF ABRAHAM LINCOLN, OF SPRINGFIELD TOWNSHIP, CHESTER COUNTY, PENNSYLVANIA.

The records contain important traces also of the children of Abraham Lincoln, of Springfield, Chester County, Pennsylvania. As we have seen from the will of Abraham, he left the following children: Mordecai, Abraham, Isaac, John and Sarah. Mordecai is mentioned in the will as absent from home, John and Sarah as minors. The testator seems particularly solicitous about his young son, John, as may be seen in the wording of the special provisions of the will in his case. One can read between the lines the father's anxiety as to the boy's reaching his maturity. In case he grows to manhood, the testator directs that a proper house be constructed for his son John. The specifications as to the size and quality of this house are very precise. It must be seventeen feet square, two stories high, and have a cedar roof.

The first document so far found referring to Abraham Lincoln, the son of Abraham of Springfield, is a deed dated May 1, 1744, in which John Fordham and his wife Hannah, of the city of Philadelphia, convey a piece of ground on the north side of Jones' alley, in the city of Philadelphia, to "Abraham Lincon of the same city cordwainer." That this Abraham was not the Abraham of Springfield, but the son of the latter, is clear from the fact that he is called "cordwainer" and mentioned as living in Philadelphia. This is further corroborated by a deed of "Abraham Lincon cordwainer" to "Isaac Lincon Carpenter" dated May 1, 1745, after the death of Abraham of Springfield. The deed of 1744 runs thus:

THIS INDENTURE Made the first Day of May in the year of our Lord one thousand seven hundren and forty four. Between John Fordham late of the City of Philadelphia but now of the Island of Jamaica Upholsterer. and Hannah Fordham of the City of Philadelphia aforesaid Wife of the said John Fordham. of the one part and Abraham Lincoln of the same City Cordwainer of the other Part.

Whereas Abraham Bickley late of Burlington in the Western Division of the Province of New Jersey. Merchant deceased Father of the Said Hannah Ford— by his Last Will and Testament in Writing duly executed bearing Date the thirteenth Day of October in the Year of our Lord one thousand seven hundred and Twenty five did Give & Bequeath unto his Daughter Hannah. divers Lands Tenements & Hereditaments (of which the Piece of Ground herein after particularly mentioned & described is Part) To hold to the said Hannah. her Heirs & Assigns for ever. Under the yearly Quitrent & Reservations accruing to the Proprietor for the same as by the said Will since duly proved Reference being had thereto more fully may appear. [Here follows Letter of Attorney]

And whereas the said Hannah Fordham hath by Virtue of the said Letter of Attorney from the said John Fordham her Husband as well as in her own Right contracted and agreed with the said Abraham Lincon for the Sale of the Fee Simple and Inheritance of the said Piece of Ground herein after particularly described Subject to the Rent herein after mentioned and to indemnify the same And the said Abraham Lincon his Heirs Executors and Administrators of and from the Payment of the said Mortgage Money and Every Part thereof.

Now this Indenture Witnesseth that now in Pursuance of such Agreement as aforesaid And for and in Consideration of the Payment of the Rent and Performance of the Covenants hereinafter reserved and contained on the Part and Behalf of the said Abraham Lincon his Heirs and Assigns to be paid done and performed They the said John Fordham by his said Attorney the said Hannah his Wife have granted bargained sold released and confirmed and by these presents do grant bargain sell release and confirm unto the said Abraham Lincon His Heirs and Assigns all that Piece of Ground situate on the North side of Jones's Alley in the City of Philadelphia aforesaid containing in Front on the said alley thirty three feet and Seven Inches and extending back or Northward Thirty Foot Bounded Eastward with other Ground of the said John Fordham and Hannah his Wife now in the Possession of George Harding Southward with the said Alley. Westward with other Ground of the said John Fordham, and

Hannah his Wife and Northward with the Ground formerly belonging to James Porbuee * * * Yielding and Paying heretofore unto the said John Fordham and Hannah his Wife and to his Heirs and Assigns of the said Hannah the yearly Rent or Sum of Seven Pounds Ten shillings and nine Pence lawful money of the Province of Pennsylvania aforesaid on the first day of May in each year for ever * * * * * * * * * * And also that the said Abraham Lincon his Heirs or Assigns shall & will within the space of Two Years next ensuing the Date. hereof. at his and their own proper Costs and Charges cause to be erected built and finished in or upon the said hereby granted Piece of Ground and Premises one good Tenantable Dwelling House of Brick or Stone two Stories High above ground with a cellar under the same. * * *. [Recorded April 10, 1767.]

Another important document bearing upon the sons of Abraham Lincoln, of Springfield, is a deed of mortgage dated September 14, 1747, in which "Jacob Lincon, of Kingsess [ing], in the County of Philadelphia Sithemaker and Anne his Wife and Abraham Lincon of the City of Philadelphia, cordwainer" mortgage Jacob Lincoln's plantation in Springfield township to Jacob Duché for the sum of 200 pounds. The text of the document follows:

"Be it Remembered that the fourteenth Day of September Anno Dom 1747 the Mortgage hereafter mentioned was produced Before Thomas

Greene Esq[r] one of the Provincial Iudges and thereupon Came Jacob Lincon and Anne his Wife and Abraham Lincon who acknowledged the s[d] Writing to be their Deed and Desired y[e] same might be recorded the s[d] Anne thereunto Voluntarily Consenting she being of full age Secretly and apart Examined and the contents of y[e] s[d] Writing read unto her w[ch] said Mortgage is recorded in y[e] Office for recording of Deed in y[e] s[d] County the Thirtieth Day of October Anno Dom 1747 in these Words (viz)

THIS INDENTURE made the fourteenth Day of September in the Year of our Lord one thousand seven hundred and forty seven Between Jacob Lincon of Kingsess in the County of Philadelphia Sithemaker and Anne his Wife and Abraham Lincon of the City of Philadelphia Cordwainer of the one part and Jacob Duche of the City of Philadelphia Merch[t] of the other part WHEREAS the s[d] Jacob Lincon in and by a Certain Obligation or Writing Obligatory under his hand and seal bearing Even Date herewith standeth Bound unto the s[d] Jacob Duch'e in the sum of Two hundred Pounds Lawfull money of Pennsylvania conditioned for the Payment of one hundred pounds Lawful money aforesaid Together with Lawfull Interest for y[e] same in manner following, to say * * *

Ye said Jacob Lincon and Anne his Wife and Abraham Lincon * * * Have Granted Bargained sold released and Confirmed and by these Psents [sic] do Grant Bargain Sell release and Confirm unto y[e] s[d] Jacob Duch'e and to his heirs and assigns All that his ye s^d Jacob Lincon's Messuage Plantation and Tract of Land thereunto Belonging Situate in Springfield Township in ye County of Chester Lying on the South West side of ye road Leading from Springfield Meeting House to the Burrough of Chester & Lying between the s^d road & Crum Creek and extending from the said Creek by Bartholomew Coppocks Land North fifty five Degrees Easterly to the afores^d road and from ye said Road to the s^d Creek south fifty five degrees West by George Lownes Land Containing one hundred and eighty acres or there about be the same more or less (which Abraham Lincon ye farther of ye s^d Abraham and Jacob Parties hereto by his Last Will and Testament of the 15th Day of April 1745 Devised unto this s^d son Iacob in ffee * * *''

[Recorded in the Court House, West Chester Pa.]

An indenture, dated February 14, 1754, informs us concerning a third son of Abraham Lincoln, of Springfield, namely, Isaac Lincoln, who with his wife, Mary, conveyed to George Westcott of the same city, brazier, a certain piece of ground willed by Abraham Lincoln of Springfield to his son Isaac, and situated on the south side of Elbow lane. This same document gives important information as to Mordecai Lincoln, the absent son of Abraham of Springfield. It appears here that Mordecai did not return within the seven years allowed by the will, nor at any time afterwards up to the date of this deed, a period of nearly ten years. Thus the property willed to Mordecai was divided between Abraham and Isaac Lincoln, as directed by their father's will. The text of the indenture follows below:

THIS INDENTURE Made the Fourteenth day of February in the year of our Lord one thousand seven Hundred and fifty four Between Isaac Lincon of the City of Philadelphia Carpenter and Mary his wife of the one part and George Wescott of the said City Brazier of the other part Whereas in and by a certain Indenture bearing date the twenty ninth day of March in the Year 1744 between William Clare of the said City of Philadelphia Cordwainer of the one part and Abraham Lincon of Springfield in the County of Chester Yeoman who was the father of the said Isaac Lincon of the other part reciting as therein is recited he / the said William Clare for the consideration therein mentioned did grant release and confirm unto the said Abraham Lincon A Certain messuage or tenement and lot or piece of ground situate in the City on the South side of Elbow Lane &c. * * * * and the said Abraham being so thereof seized and did make his last will and testament in writing bearing date the fifteenth day of April 1745 and therein divided All that messuage or tenement which he purchased of William Clare situate in the said City unto the said testators son Mordecai if he returned into the Province of Pennsylvania within the term of seven years to hold to him the said Mordecai his heirs and assigns forever But if it should happen that his son Mordecai shall not return before the expiration of the term of seven

years aforesaid then the testators will is and he
doth give the said Messuage & testament unto
his said son Isaac his heirs and assigns forever Provided nevertheless that his son Isaac
pay or cause to be paid unto the said Mordecai if in case he returns at any time after
the seven years aforesaid the sum of five pounds
lawful money of Pennsylvania as [at?] in and
by the said last recited Indenture and last will
relation being thereunto had respectively appears and shortly after the making of the testament aforesaid he the said testator died And
the said Mordecai did not return into the said
Province within the term aforesaid limited nor at
any time since So that the estate in the premises
is vested in the said Isaac Lincon as divided by
the Instrument aforesaid Subject nevertheless to
the payment of the said five pounds unto the said
Mordecai if in case he shall hereafter arrive in
the said Province Now this indenture witnesseth that the said Isaac Lincon and Mary his wife
for and in consideration of the sum of sixty five
pounds lawful money of Pennsylvania unto them
well and truly paid by the said George Wescott
* * * do bargain sell * * * A certain
piece of ground being the westermost part of the
aforesaid thirty seven foot * * * bounded
northward with Elbow Lane &c * * *

Isaac Lincon
Mary Lincon

[Receipt also signed by same
Acknowledged Feb 14, 1754
Recorded Apr. 29, 1835]

John Lincoln, the young son of Abraham Lincoln of Springfield, died without issue and his land passed to Abraham, his brother, and was divided by him, Abraham, between his daughters, Rebecca and Hester. Rebecca married James Carter, a merchant of Philadelphia, and Hester died young.

Isaac Lincoln, the son of Abraham of Springfield, married Mary Schute December the 30th, 1746. Jacob Lincoln, son of Abraham of Springfield, married Ann Rambo, June, 1747. Jacob died June 5, 1769, aged 44 years, and was buried at Kingsessing Swedes Church.

In Old Swedes Church, Philadelphia (O. S. C. P.), First Baptist Church, Philadelphia (F. B. C. P.), St. Michael's and Zion Churches, and in Christ Church, Philadelphia (C. C. P.), we find the following records of Lincoln marriages, which we arrange here in chronological order, with the reference to the church in parenthesis:

Lincoln, Daniel, and Mary Medley, June 2, 1742

Lincon, Isaac, and Mary Shute, Dec. 31, 1746 (C. C. P.).

Jacob Lincoln and Ann Rambo, June 1747. Jacob died June 5 1769 aged 44 years, buried at Old Swedes, Kingsessing. Anne died Feb. 8, 1819, aged 94 years, buried at same place.

Children: Moses, Catarina (b. June 16. 1751), John (b. Feb. 1, 1756, m. Elizabeth Neal or O'Neal Oct 8, 1781), Rebecca (b. Dec. 11, 1757), Mary (b. Aug. 17, 1763), Jacob (b. Apr. 1766).

Lincon, Rebecca, and Joseph Rush, Sept. 19, 1750
(C. C. P.).

Lincoln, Rebecca, and James Carter, Mar. 7, 1763
(F. B. C. P.).

Lincoin, Margaret, and James Gregory, July 17,
1769 (C. C. P.).

Lincon, Sarah, and Samuel Pastorius, Nov. 28,
1771

John Linkhorn and Elizabeth O'Neal Oct. 8, 1781
(O. S. C. P.).

Barbara Kinch

. Lincorn, Elizabeth, and John Hart, July 7, 1791
(O. S. C. P.).

Lincoln, Jacob, and Mary Taylor, April 11, 1792
(O. S. C. P.).

Lincoin, Moses, and Barbara Kinch, Mar. 19,
1795 (O. S. C. P.).

Lincoln, Benjamin, and Ann Cowan, May 19,
1806 (C. C. P.).

The Parish Register of Christ Church, Philadelphia, contains the following:

"Christenings 1735 Aug 3. Mordecai Son of Abraham and Rebecca Lincoln age 15
years"

"1748 April 13 Lincoln, negro slave of Robert
Grove adult"

"1749 Feb. 11 John son of John & Catharine Lincoln born Dec^br 17. 1749"

CHAPTER V.

CHILDREN OF MORDECAI LINCOLN OF EXETER.

Having followed the traces of Abraham Lincoln of Springfield and his children in the counties of Chester and Philadelphia, we return to Mordecai Lincoln of Exeter and trace his family in Berks County, Pennsylvania, and in Virginia and Kentucky, down to Abraham Lincoln, the President of the United States.

It will be remembered that Mordecai Lincoln of Exeter, Pennsylvania, son of Mordecai of Hull, Massachusetts, provided in his will for three sons, Mordecai, John and Thomas, and conditionally for a posthumous child. This posthumous child, as the documents will show, was born Oct. 18 (O. S.), or Oct. 29 (N. S.), 1736, after his father's death, named Abraham and received his share of his father's estate in accordance with the provisions of the will. Mordecai of Exeter made his surviving wife, Mary, his executrix and appointed his friends, Jonathan Robeson and George Boone, to assist her in settling the estate.

MORDECAI LINCOLN, SON OF MORDECAI OF EXETER.

The earliest references to Mordecai Lincoln, son of Mordecai of Exeter, show him to be unmarried.

In the tax lists of Berks County his name appears as follows:

			£	£	s	d	Township
Single	1754	Mordecai Lincoln		9			Exeter
	1757	Marthicai Lingcoln and half tenement	20				Exeter
	1758	Mordecai Lincoln Tent ½	20				Exeter
		Special Assessment for the same year	10				
Married	1759	Lincoln, Mordecai	10		15		Exeter
	1759	Mordecai Lincoln (County Tax)	12				
	1760	Lincoln, Mordecai	15				Exeter
	1761	Lincoln, Mordecai	15		3	9	Exeter
	1763	Lincoln, Mordecai	22		5		Exeter
	1765	Lincoln, Mordecai	21	1	11	6	Exeter
	1766	Lincoln, Mordecai	18		4	6	Exeter

The name of Mordecai Lincoln (or "Lincorn") appears frequently in the old manuscript account book kept by Abraham Lincoln, his brother, from 1755 to 1778. On the first page of this book is written:

Abram Lincoln| Beginning to Doy et at| Mordecai Lincorns yᵉ 21ᵗʰ of yᵉ third month| In the year 1757.

The following entries appear at different times during this year 1757 and later:

Mordecai Lincoln D^r| to four Days mak-
  ing Shingels
Mordecai Lincoln| to two days and a ½
  Reaping   £o 5s 6d
Mordecai Licln to one days work   o 2 o
Mordecai Lincoln for one days work   o 2 o
Mordecai Lincoln to one days work   o 2 o
  and cash   [?]
Mordecai Lincoln to one ½ days work   o 1 o
Mordecai Lincoln to ⅔ of a days work o 1 6
Mordecai Lin [coln] to work
Mordecai Lincoln to 3 days and a half
  work   o 7 o
Mordecai Lincoln to One days sawing Jn
  exchange of Work
Mordecai Lincoln to Cash   o 2 o
1759, May Mordecai Lincoln to a Half a
  bushel of flax sade   o 2 6
June Mordecai Lincoln to three Bushel
  of Buck Wheat   6
1770 April y^e 10th C^r
  Mordecai Lincoln
  C^r by work at the Rase
  apil [sic] 10th by 2½ days work
  April y^e 14th no [=anno] 1770 Cr by work
    on the Rods
  Mordecai Lincoln 1 hand
  Mordecai Lincoln Mikel Syser & Jacob
    Battle is to Maintane two Thirds of y^e
    Rase from y^e first of march to the Six-
    teenth of October yere af ter yer
  1778 October Cr by work dune at the Ras
  24th Mordecai Lincoln 1 hand

1779

April 3

Mordeca [sic] two hand one d day & Self prt"

The land records of Berks County contain reference to a number of transactions of Mordecai Lincoln, as the following list will show:

> Grantor Mordecai Lincoln, Oct. 16, 1766, Grantee William Tallman, Asst., book 6, page 330.
>
> Grantee Mordecai Lincoln, Apr. 11, 1769, Grantors Abraham et al., Exeter, book 14, page 543.
>
> Grantor Mordecai Lincoln, Apr. 11, 1769, Grantee Jacob Bechtel, Exeter, book 14, page 545.
>
> Grantor Mordecai Lincoln, Apr. 11, 1769, Grantee Michael Seyster (= Zeister), Release, book 15, page 5.
>
> Grantee Mordecai Lincoln, May 9, 1769, Grantors Thomas and Abraham Lincoln, Exeter, book 11, page 307.
>
> Grantors Mordecai & Abraham Lincoln, May 16, 1770, Grantee Michael Zeister, Exeter, book 6, page 504.
>
> Grantor Mordecai Lincoln, Mar. 29, 1773, Grantee Mary Rogers, Sch. River, book 1B, page 535.
>
> Grantor Mordecai Lincoln, May 22, 1784, Grantee Jno. Spohn, Exeter, book 9 ,page 54.
>
> Grantor Mordecai Lincoln, Oct. 30, 1784, Grantee Henry Huyett, Ex. Com. Bk. P., book 1, page 163.
>
> Grantors Mordecai Lincoln et al., July 4, 1789, Grantee Rebecca Nagle, Exeter, book 12, page 4.

There is a reference to Mordecai Lincoln in the deed books of Berks County, Pennsylvania, showing that he and his wife, Mary, conveyed to Mary Rogers, of Reading, a certain property originally belonging to the estate of his father Mordecai Lincoln of Exeter. The deed which is dated March 29, 1773, begins and ends as follows:

> THIS INDENTURE Made the 29th day of March in the year of our Lord one thousand seven hundred and seventy three BETWEEN Mordecai Lin-

coln of Exeter Township in Berks County and Province of Pennsylvania Yeoman and Mary his Wife of the one part and Mary Rogers of the Town of Reading in ye County and province aforesaid Widow of the other part [Here follows the recital of the title, the essential part of which runs: "And the said Thomas Millard and Barbara his Wife by Jndentures of Lease & release bearing date the 9th & 10th days of May Anno domini 1730 did grant and Confirm the same One Thousand acres of land and premises unto the said Mordecai Lincoln the Elder in fee [then follows the recital of the will of Mordecai Lincoln of Exeter, "the elder" and the conditions of sale by Mordecai Lincoln (Junior) and his wife Mary to Mary Rogers]

```
                 her
        Mary  M  Lincoln          (Seal)
                mark
        MORDECAI LINCOLN          (Seal)*
```

In the Account Books of John Harris we find this interesting entry:

```
1785 Linkhorn in Town Dr.            £ s d
June 1st To Sundries brought from
              Folio 169                6 8 7
        To 27 Bundles Rye Straw Lent
```

May 21 1790 Recd the opposite acco^t in full £6.8.7.

This was evidently Mordecai Lincoln, son of Mordecai of Exeter, who appears in a deed dated July 4, 1789, as a resident of Dauphin County, Pa. Mordecai settled later in Fayette County, Pa.

---

* Cf. Deed Book I. B., 535 et seq., Reading, Pa.

THOMAS LINCOLN, SON OF MORDECAI OF EXETER.

The second son of Mordecai Lincoln, the elder, of Exeter, was Thomas Lincoln, who took a prominent part in the affairs of Berks County, Pennsylvania. His name appears in the early tax lists with the following assessments:

Berks Co. Tax List	£	£	s.	d.	Township
1757 Thomas Lingorn	6				Amity
1758 Thomas Lincoln	16		4		Exeter
1758 Thomas Lincoln	15				
his Tennant	5				
	20	1	10		Exeter
1759 Lincoln Thomas	7		10	6	Reading
1759 Lincoln Thomas	15	1	2	6	Exeter
1760 Tho' Lincoln	9				Reading
1760 Lincoln Thomas	6	9			Reading

In 1758 he was made sheriff of Berks County, a fact which strangely enough escaped the officials of the same county some years ago, when they had the calendar of sheriffs printed, but omitted the name of Thomas Lincoln. The present writer had the peculiar pleasure of rediscovering Sheriff Thomas Lincoln and identifying his signature in old lists of jurors returned by him while sheriff. The original bond given by Thomas Lincoln, as newly elected Sheriff to the King, is duly recorded* and may be reprinted here as a document of interest:

KNOW ALL MEN by these Presents that We Thomas Lincoln of Exeter Township in the

---

* In Commission Book A No. 2, p. 268-9. (Department of Internal Affairs, Harrisburg, Pa.)

The King

                    }
or

Elisabeth Crowl.

Bill of Costs

Judges & Clerk	4. 6. 0		
Attorney General	1. 16. 0		
Sheriff	1. 00. 0		
Jury	0. 11. 0		9 11 6
Summoning Adam Sorrick & Wife	0. 11. 6		
their attendance 3 days each	0. 12. 0		
Ringing the Bell	0. 05. 0		
Cryers fees	0. 10. 0		
The Hire of 10 hands one day at	10. 0		
Building the Gaol at 5/ pr day			
To one Rope	0. 04. 0		11 9 0
To Cash paid the Hang Man	7. 10. 0		
To the Expence of Keeping him 11.5.0 x 18.0			21 0 6
To Sundry Other expenses Concerning the Execution of the said Crowl	2. 0. 0		

Tho. Lincoln Sh.

BILL OF COSTS OF EXECUTING ELISABETH CROWL.
(Original in the Possession of Louis Richards, of Reading, Pa.)

County of Berks Esq' Jsaac Levan of Exeter aforesaid Gent. and William Boone of the same place Gent. are held and firmly bound unto our Sovereign Lord George the second by the Grace of God of Great Britain France and Ireland King Defender of the Faith &c^a in the Sum of three hundred Pounds Current Money of Pennsylvania to be paid to our said Sovereign Lord the King his Heirs or Successors to which Payment well and truly to be maide We do find our Selves each and every or any of Us for and in the Whole our each and every or any of our Heirs Executors and Administrators respectively Jointly and Severally firmly by these Presents Sealed WITH our Seals Dated the fifth Day of October in the thirty second year of the Reign of our said Lord the King & in the Year of our Lord one thousand and seven hundred and fifty-eight.

THE CONDITION of this obligation is such That WHEREAS the above bounden Thomas Lincoln on the second Day of October Jnstant was Elected Sheriff for the said County of Berks for the ensuing Year by the Freemen of the said County according to an Act of Assembly of this Province passed in the fourth year of the Reign of Queen Ann entitled an Act for Regulating Elections of Sheriffs & Coroners As by a certain Jndenture bearing Date the second Day of October Jnstant made or mentioned to be made BETWEEN Thomas Lincoln Coroner of the said County of the one Part & Joseph Boone Sebastian Levan Mounce Jones Benjamin Talbert Ganis Dickinson & Henry Snyder Freeholders of the said County

of the other Part Gentlemen Freeholders of the
Said County of the other Part Relation bearing
thereunto had appears NOW if the said Thomas
Lincoln by himself or his Lawful Deputy shall
and do well and truly perform his Duty & Trust
in the said office of Sheriff when thereunto lawfully and thoroughly Qualified according to the
Tenor of the Affirmation which he shall make
for the due Execution of his said Office Or else
to be and remain in full Force and Virtue to the
Uses Jntents and Purposes in the said Act—mentioned and appointed And to no other Use Jntent
or Purpose whatsoever Thomas Lincoln (Seal)
Jsaac Levan (Seal) Willm Boone (Seal) Sealed
and Delivered in the Presence of Us C. Brockden,
Robt Harper. Acknowledged at Philadelphia the
fifth day of October A°. D^l. 1758 Before me W^m
Coleman, Recorded 6th Day of October, 1758.

The records of the Prothonotary's office in Reading contain many papers executed by Thomas Lincoln during his term as sheriff. The accompanying
list of jurors* and the very interesting case of the
hanging of a woman, will serve as specimens, both
of his work and of his signature.

The following transactions of Thomas Lincoln
appear in the land records of Berks County,
Pennsylvania:

---

* The "List of Jurors" was found by the co-operation of
the Prothonotary and his aides. The original of the execution account is in the possession of Louis Richards, Esq., of
Reading, President of the Bucks County Historical Society,
who kindly permitted the writer to have it photographed.

List of Petit Jury Return'd
to serve at August Term

1. Isaac Levan, Jun.
2. Timothy Millard
3. John Hunter
4. John Rhoads
5. Isaac Wickersham
6. George Gernand
7. Michael Bright
8. Paul Leboe
9. Francis Winrick
10. John Wilman
11. William Miller
12. Thomas Prall
13. Peter Baum
14. Jacob Baldy
15. Nicholas Mertz
16. Philip Weiser
17. Anthony Fisher
18. John Hartman
19. Mathias Sowermilch
20. Jonathan Millard
21. Joseph Kurtz
22. Davis Evans, Jun.
23. Thomas Wilton
24. W. Cox Bicfer

Summoned pr Me

Tho. Lincoln Sher.

LIST OF PETIT JURY RETURNED BY THOMAS
LINCOLN, SHERIFF OF READING, PA.

Grantor Thomas Lincoln, Dec. 29, 1757, Grantee William
Tallman, Schuylkill, book 6, page 327.
Grantor Thomas Lincoln, Feb. 15, 1759, Grantee Richard
Wistar, Hereford, book 5, page 373.
Grantor Thomas Lincoln, Nov. 4, 1760, Grantee Michael
Zeister, Exeter, book 2, page 178.
Grantee Thomas Lincoln, Sept. 9, 1761, Grantor Hans
Adam Epler, Reading, book 9, page 435.
Grantor Thomas Lincoln, Nov. 14, 1761, Grantee Adam
Scheier, Reading, book 3B, page 265.
Grantee Thomas Lincoln, May 14, 1762, Grantor David
Henderson, Reading, book 4, page 265.
Grantor Thomas Lincoln, Nov. 28, 1763, Grantee Jacob
Rowbold, Reading, book 9, page 437.
Grantor Thomas Lincoln, Mar. 14, 1764, Grantee Conrad
Bower, Reading, book 4, page 267.
Grantee Thomas Lincoln, May 4, 1774, Grantor Mary
Rogers, Discharge, book 1B, page 536.

The following document gives us a specimen
of the business transactions of Thomas Lincoln,
Sheriff:

To ALL PEOPLE to whom these Presents shall
come I Thomas Lincoln late Sheriff of the County
of Berks in the province of Pennsylvania send
Greeting WHEREAS by a writ of Fieri Facias to
me directed bearing Teste the Fifteenth Day of
February in the Thirty second Year of the King's
Reign (1759) issuing out of the Court of Common Pleas of the County aforesaid I was Com-
manded That of the Goods and Chattels Lands
and Tenements which were of Rudolph Berkey
late of the said County Yeoman deceased otherwise lately called Rudolph Pierge of Maxataneya
twship Philadelpa County Yeoman at the Time of

his Death in the hands of Richard Wistar late of my County Merchant Acting Executor of the last Will and Testament of the said Rudolph Berkey in my Bailiwick I should Cause to be levied as well a Certain Debt of One Thousand Pounds lawful Money of Pennsylvania * * * * Now Know ye that I the said Thomas Lincoln late Sheriff of the County of Berks aforesaid for and in consideration of the aforesaid Sum of One thousand and Ten pounds unto me well and truly paid by the said Richard Wistar at and before the ensealing and delivery hereof the Receipt whereof I do hereby Acknowledge and thereof do Acquit and for ever discharge the said Richard Wistar his Heirs Executors and Administrators by these presents have granted bargained Sold Aliened released and Confirmed And by force and Virtue of the last recited Writ and of the Laws of this province in such Case made and provided DO grant bargain sell alien release and Confirm unto the said Richard Wistar and to his Heirs and Assigns All those the above described Messuage *
* * * * * * * * * * * * * *

In the deed of Thomas Lincoln to Michael Zeister we have important information of Thomas Lincoln's land:

This Jndenture made the fourth Day of November in the Year of Our Lord one thousand seven hundred and sixty Between Thomas Lin-

---

* Deed Book 5, p. 373 et seq., Recorder's Office, Reading, Pa.

coln of the Town of Reading in the County of
Berks in the Province of Pennsylvania Esquire
and Elizabeth his Wife of the one part And
Michael Zeister of the same Place Sadler of the
other part Witnesseth that the said Thomas Lincoln and Elizabeth his Wife for and in Consideration of the Sum of one thousand pounds lawful Money of Pennsylvania to them in hand paid
by the said Michael Zeister the receipt whereof
is hereby acknowledged have given granted aliened released enfeoffed and confirmed and by
these presents do give grant bargain and sell
alien release enfeoff and confirm unto the said
Michael Zeister and his heirs a certain Tract and
parcel of Land situated in Exeter Township in
Berks County aforesaid Bounded by the following lines to wit * * * * thence by Land of Abraham Lincoln and other Land of the said William Tallman * * * * Containing by Computa-
tion three hundred and three acres be the same
more or less [Being part of a Tract of one thousand Acres of Land which Tobias Collet Daniel
Quair and Henry Goldey by Deed Dated the twentyeth day of February Anno Domini 1718 granted
to a certain Andrew Robeson in ffee And which
the said Andrew Robeson by his Last Will
devised to his son Jonathan Robeson in ffee
* * * and which the said Jonathan Robeson
by Deed Dated the twenty seventh day of October Anno Domini 1729 granted to a certain
Thomas Willard in ffee And which the said
Thomas Millard by Deed DATED DATED the tenth

day of May Anno Domini 1730 granted to Mordecai Lincoln (the Father of the said Thomas Lincoln) in ffee One third part of which One-Thousand-Acre-Tract the said Mordecai Lincoln by his Last Will and Testament dated the twenty second day of February Anno Domini 1735 * * * * * * * * * * * * * * * *

Tho. Lincoln   (Seal)
Elizabeth Lincoln   (Seal)*

The following refer to sales of property made to or by Thomas Lincoln in Reading:

This Jndenture Made the fourteenth Day of November in the year of our Lord one thousand Seven Hundred & sixty one Between Thomas Lincoln of the town of Reading in the County of Berks and province of Pennsylvania Gentleman and Elizabeth his wife of the one part and Adam Scheir of the said town of Reading Carpenter of the other part Whereas the Honble Thomas Penn & Richard Penn Esquires Proprietories in * * * * 1752 did Give Grant Release and confirm unto a Certain Francis Morgan * * * * Lot of Ground situate in the Town of Reading aforesaid and Marked in the General Plan of the said Town Nº 404 * * * *

And Whereas the said Francis Morgan and Jane his wife by Deed indented under their Hands and Seals bearing date the thirteenth day of November in the year of our Lord one thousand

---

* Deed Book 2, 175 ff., in Recorder's office, Reading, Pa.

seven hundred and sixty one for the Consideration therein Mentioned did Grant and Confirm unto a Certain Thomas Lincoln and to his Heirs and Assigns All that the above Mentioned and Described Lot of Ground N° 404 With the Appurtenances &c*

THIS INDENTURE made the Fourteenth Day of March in the Year of our Lord one Thousand Seven Hundred and Sixty four BETWEEN Thomas Lincoln of Reading in Berks County and Province of Pennsylvania Mason and Elizabeth his Wife of the one part And Conrad Bower of the same Place Inn Keeper of the other part &c.**

[Consideration 130 pounds, 7½ acres.]

Thomas Lincoln appears also, even more frequently than Mordecai his elder brother, in the old Account Book of Abraham Lincoln, their youngest brother, as the following entries will show:

	£	s	d
1756 Thomas Lincoln to 3 days work at 2 s Pr day	0	6	0
Thomas Lincoln Cᵣ by one Quir and a ½ of Paper	0	1	0
Thoˢ Lincoln to one day and a half	0	3	0
Thoˢ Lincoln fife days and a halfs work Dt	0	11	0
Thoˢ Lincoln to one weeks Work	0	12	0
Thoˢ Lincoln to one day and ½ halfs work	0	3	0

---

* Deed Book 3 B, pp. 265 et seq.
** Deed Book 4, pp. 267 et seq.

Thos Lincoln to one days work	o	2	o
Thos Lincoln Dt for work	o	1	o
Thos Lincoln to Cash Lent	o	?	?
Thos Lincoln dt upon Ballans			
March ye first	o	o	7
Thos Lincoln to sawing 6 foot	o	1	3
1758 Thos Lincoln to sawing 5 days at			

s   d

at 2.. 6 per Day	o	12	6
Decmbr 30 Thos Lincoln to one			
half Days work	o	1	o
Jany Thos Lincoln to one			
Days wriding [writing?]	o	2	6

ABRAHAM LINCOLN, SON OF MORDECAI OF EXETER.

The third son of Mordecai Lincoln, the elder, of
Exeter, was John Lincoln, or "Virginia John," as
tradition has handed down his name. Inasmuch as
it is through him that the migration of the Lincoln
family is continued into Virginia and in his descendants to Kentucky, it will be more convenient to treat
him last and to consider his youngest brother, Abraham, next before leaving the traces of the family in
Pennsylvania.

The records of Abraham Lincoln, the posthumous
son of Mordecai the elder, of Exeter, and his descendants are preserved fortunately in an old family
book, or "Lincoln Record," as we shall call it
here. This book, still preserved in manuscript, is
one of the precious heirlooms of the descendants of
Abraham Lincoln. The MS. contains, in the first
part, the record of the family of Abraham Lincoln

FIRST PAGE OF THE ACCOUNT BOOK OF ABRAHAM LINCOLN, OF EXETER.
(Original in the Possession of Richard Lincoln, of Reading, Pa.)

and, in the second part, the record of the Boone family.* The Record appears to have been first kept by posthumous Abraham Lincoln, then by his sons Mordecai and Thomas, and then by Thomas' son, John D. Lincoln and others. It was copied some years ago by Harrison P. Lincoln, who had blue prints made and furnished a number of them to libraries and individuals.

The Lincoln Record is very precise in its data, as the entries, concerning Abraham Lincoln and Anna Boone, his wife, will show. The text of the Lincoln part of the "Lincoln Record" is printed in full at the end of this chapter.

The name of Abraham Lincoln, the posthumous son of Mordecai, the elder, of Exeter, like that of his brothers, appears in the tax lists of Berks County, Pennsylvania, as the following, taken from the originals, now found in the possession of the Berks County Historical Society, will show:

---

*A fragmentary record of the Boone family in the handwriting of the Lincoln Record is still extant in loose sheets in the possession of Louis Richards, President of the Berks County Historical Society. It contains the following interesting notes:

"Daniel Boone [son of Squire & Sarah Boone] was born October, A. D. 1733.

He and the Rest of their Family left Exeter on the 1 May 1750, and moved to North Carolina, where they settled. But at present he is settled on the Ohio at Kentucky.

1781 October 20. Then Daniel came to see us, the first Time.

1788 February 12. Then Daniel Boone (with Rebecca his Wife & their Son Nathan) came to see us. Died at Charette Village in Missouri on the 26 of Sept. 1820."

		£	£	s.	d.	Township
1758	Abraham Lincoln					
	[Single Men]		1			
	(Special Assessment)					
1759	Lincoln Abram					Exeter
1759	Abram Lincorn					
	[Single Men]					
1760	Lincoln Abram	18	1	7		Exeter
1761	Lincoln, Abram*		9			Exeter
1763	Lincoln Abram	20	5			Exeter
1765	Lincoln Abraham	19	1	8	6	Exeter
1766	Lincoln Abram	18		4	6	Exeter

The following entries of transactions of Abraham Lincoln appear in the land records:

Grantor Abraham Lincoln, Dec. 29, 1757, Grantee William Tallman, Sch. River, book 2B, page 43.

Grantors Abraham Lincoln et al., Apr. 11, 1769, Grantee Mordecai Lincoln, book 14, page 543.

Grantors Thomas and Abraham Lincoln, May 9, 1769, Grantee Mordecai Lincoln, Exeter, book 11, page 307.

Grantor Abraham Lincoln, May 26, 1769, Grantee William Tallman, Exeter, book 7, page 195.

The first of these documents gives such important information that it seemed well to print it here. From it we learn the title to the land before Mordecai, the elder, of Exeter bought it, and also the fact that Abraham Lincoln was the posthumous son of Mordecai, the elder:

---

* This assessment was probably made in 1760, as the Lincoln Record says Abraham Lincoln married Anna Boone July 10, 1760.

THIS INDENTURE Made the twenty ninth day of December in the Year of our Lord one thousand seven hundred and fifty seven BETWEEN Abraham Lincoln of Exeter in the County of Berks In the Province of Pennsylvania Yeoman of the one part and William Tallman of the same place Weaver of the other part WHEREAS by Certain Indentures of Lease and Release dated the Nineteenth and Twentieth days of February in the Year of our Lord one thousand seven hundred & Eighteen made between Tobias Collet Citizen and Haberdasher of London Daniel Quair of London and Henry Goldney of London Linnen Draper of one part and Andrew Robison then of Roxburrow in the County of Philadelphia Yeoman of the Other part and Recorded in Philad^a. in Book H Coll. 4. page 118 & they the said Tobias Collet Daniel Quair, and Henry Goldney for the Consideration therein Mentioned Confirmed unto the said Andrew Robison in ffee A Certain Tract of Land Lying on the East side of the River Schuylkill in Philadelp^a. County Beginning at a Beech tree by the said River Schuylkill and Running thence North twenty degrees East four hundred and twenty Perches to a Corner Stone thence North Seventy degrees West ffour hundred and twenty perches to a post then South Twenty Degrees West two hundred and Ninty Perches to a Hickery Tree marked Standing on the Bank of the said River then down the same on ye Several Courses thereof to the place of beginning Containing one thousand Acres of Land [and a Certain Tract of Six Hun-

dred Acres Lying on the West Side of Schuylkill
with the Appurtenances] The said Two Tracts of
Land to be holden by the said Andrew Robison
his heirs and Assigns Under the Yearly Quit Rent
of one Bever Skin on the first day of March forever AND the said Andrew Robison being So
Seized of the said Premises Dyed did by his Last
Will and Testament bearing date Anno Domi 1719
Give unto his third Son Jonathan Robison the
above Described one thousand Acres of Land with
ye Appurtenances AND Whereas Andrew Robison
Eldest Son and heir at Law of the said Andrew
Robison the Testator in and by a Deed Poll under
his hand and Seal duly Executed for ye Consideration Therein Mentioned did Grant Release Quit
Claim and Confirm unto the said Jonathan Robison all the said one thousand Acres of Land with
the Appurtenances To HOLD to him the said Jonathan Robison His Heirs and Assigns forever as
by the said Deed dated the tenth day of January
A: D: 1726 may Appear AND WHEREAS by Certain Indentures of Lease & Release Tripartite made
between Jonathan Robison and Elizabeth his wife
of the first part Mordecai Lincoln of ye second
part and Thomas Millard of ye third part the
said Jonathan Robison & Elizabeth his Wife
and Mordecai Lincoln by Indentures of
Lease and Release dated the Sixth and Seventh
days of Octobed 1729 did Confirm ye said one
thousand Acres of Land unto Thomas Millard in
ffee AND the said Thomas Millard and Barbara his
Wife by Indentures of Lease and Release dated

the Ninth and tenth days of May A°. D°. 1730 did Confirm the same One thousand Acres of Land unto the Above Named Mordecai Lincoln ye Elder in fee and being so Seized thereof dyed WHO by his Last Will and Testament dated the 22 day of February A: D: 1735 and Registered in ye Registers Office in Philad^a. June 7. 1736 did give and Bequeath unto his Son Abraham Lincoln [Party to these Presents] the one third Part of the said one thousand Acres of Land to be taken from the West End thereof which hath been Amicably Done Now THIS INDENTURE WITNESSETH that the said Abraham Lincoln for and in Consideration of the Sum of Nine Pound Current Money of Pennsylvania to him in hand paid by the said William Tallman at and before ye Sealing and Delivery hereof the Receipt thereof is hereby acknowledged Hath granted bargained and Sold Aliened Enfeofed and Confirmed and by these presents doth grant bargain and Sell Alien Enfeofe & Confirm uneo the said William Tallman and to his heirs and Assigns forever A CERTAIN Messuage Tenement and Piece of Land [part of the one third part of the above Described one thousand Acres BEGINNING at an Ash tree Standing on the West bank of the Great Creek in a line of Thomas Lincolns Land thence by ye Same North Seventeen Degrees and a half East thirty one Perches to a Black Oak & a Corner thence by s^d Abraham Lincoln's Other Land the three following Courses and distances Viz. North Seventy two degrees and a half West Eight perches

to a hickory and South twenty Nine Degrees
West Thirty one perches and a half to a post
thence South Seventy two degrees and a half
East twelve perches & Six tenths to the place
of beginning Containing two Acres of Land Together with all wood Underwoods Ways Waters
Water Courses profits commodities Advantages
Hereditaments and Appurtenances whatsoever
unto the Above Described Piece of Land belonging or in any wise appertaining and the Reversion
And Reversions Remainder and Remainders
Rents Issues and Profits thereof and all the Estate Right title Jnterest Claim and Demand of
him the said Abraham Lincoln in and to the premises herein Mentioned or Intended to be Mentioned and every Part and Parcell thereof
AND the said Abraham Lincoln for himself his
heirs and Assigns doth Covenant promise and
grant unto the said William Tallman and to his
heirs and Assigns that he the said William Tallman for himself his heirs and Assigns shall have
the Sole priviledge and Power to draw and Convey [According as he his heirs or Assigns shall
think fit for the sufficient Watering the said Piece
of Land out of the Above Mentioned Great Creek
or any part of said Creek that is near the bounds
of said Two Acres of Land To HAVE AND TO
HOLD the said Messuage Tennament and Piece
of Land and all and Singular the premises And
Priviledges aforesaid and every part and Clause
thereof with the Appurtenances unto the said
William Tallman his heirs and Assigns to the only

ADMINISTRATORS' ACCOUNT OF THE ESTATE OF ABRAHAM LINCOLN, SON OF MORDECAI LINCOLN, OF EXETER. (First Page.)

ADMINISTRATORS' ACCOUNT OF THE ESTATE OF ABRAHAM LINCOLN, SON OF
MORDECAI LINCOLN, OF EXETER. (Second Page.)

proper Use and behoof of him the said William
Tallman his heirs and Assigns for Ever Under
the proportional part of the Yearly Quitrents
from hence forward accruing unto the Chief Lord
or Lords of the ffee thereof AND the said
Abraham Lincoln for himself And his heirs doth
Covenant with the said William Tallman his
heirs and Assigns that the said Abraham Lincoln and his heirs the above Mentioned Messuage
Tennament and Piece of Land Hereditament
Premises and Priviledges and every Part and
Clause thereof with the Appurtenances unto the
said William Tallman his heirs and Assigns
Against all persons whatsoever Shall Warrant
and forever Defend By these presents AND FUR-
THER that he the said Abraham Lincoln and his
heirs and every Other Person and Persons and
his and their heirs any thing having or Claiming
in the said Messuage and Piece of Land And
Priviledges above mentioned to be hereby Granted or any Part thereof shall and will at all times
hereafter upon the Reasonable Request and at
the Cost and Charges of the said William Tallman his heirs and Assigns Make do and Execute or Cause to be all and every such further &
other Lawfull and Reasonable Act and Acts
thing and things Device and Devises Conveyance
& Conveyances in the Law whatsoever for the
further and better assuring & Confirming of
yᵉ Above Mentioned Piece of Land & Priviledges
with the Appurtenances unto the said William
Tallman his heirs and Assigns forever as by his

or their Counsil Learned in the Law shall be
Reasonably Devised Advised and Required IN
WITNESS whereof the said Abraham Lincoln hath
hereunto Set his hand and Seal dated the day
and year first above writen. Abraham Lincoln
(Seal) Sealed and Delivered in the presence of
Us John Powell Benj^a. Parks Received the day of
the date of the Above Writen Indenture of the
'Above Named William Tallman The Sum of
Nine Pounds being in full the Consideration
above Mentioned J say Received Abraham Lincoln John Powell Benj^a. Park (indorsed thus) On
the Eighteenth Day of Augt. Anno Domi 1759
before me Jonas Seely Esqr. one of the Justices
&c for the County of Berks Came ye within
Named Abram Lincoln and Acknowledged the
within Indenture to be his Act and Deed and De-
sird the same May be Recorded as such in Tes-
timony where of J have hereunto Set my Hand
and Seal the Day & Date above written Jonas
Seely (Seal) (and further indorsed thus)
To ALL PEOPLE to WHOME THESE PRESENTS
SHALL COME Know YE that we Mordecai Lincoln
and Thomas Lincoln of Exeter in the County of
Berks in the Province of Pennsylvania [Sons of
Mordecai Lincoln Deceased and Within Men-
tioned] for divers good Causes and Considerations us thereunto Moving have Remised Released and forever Quit Claimed and By these
presents do Remise Release and for Ever Quit
Claim unto William Tallman [within Mentioned]
his heirs and Assigns for Ever all that Messuage

ADMINISTRATOR'S ACCOUNT OF THE ESTATE OF ANN LINCOLN, WIDOW OF ABRAHAM LINCOLN, OF EXETER.

Tenement And Piece of Land of two Acres with
the priviledges and Appurtenances and every part
thereof [Which in the Within Indenture is Speci-
fied Mentioned or Intended to be Mentioned] To
HAVE AND TO HOLD all and Singular the said Messuage Tennament and Piece of Land and Priviledge with the Appurtenances unto the said William Tallman his heirs and Assigns forever
And all the Estate Right Title Interest Claim and
Demand whatsoever of us the said Mordecai
and Thomas Lincoln and of each of us our heirs
and each of our heirs and Assigns or any Other
Person or Persons Claiming or to Claim by from
or Under us or Any of Us of in and to the
thereby Granted Premises & Privileges or any
Part thereof IN WITNESS whereof we have hereunto Jnterchangeably Set our hand & Seals This
twenty Ninth Day of December in the Year of
our Lord one thousand Seven hundred and fifty
Seven Mordecai Lincoln (Seal) Thomas Lincoln
(Seal) SEALED AND DELIVERED in the presence
of Us John Powell Benj[a]. Parks Berks County ss
Be it remembered that on the twenty fifth Day
of October Anno Domini 1774 Before me the
Subscriber One of His Majesty's Justices of the
Peace of the County of Berks Came Benjamin
Parks of the Town of Reading in the said County
Joiner and (being one of the People called Quakers) on his solemn Affirmation according to Law
did declare that he saw the Above Named Mordecai Lincoln & Thomas Lincoln Sign Seal and
as their Act and Deed respectively deliver the
above Instrument of Writing and that the Name

Benj[a]. Parks thereto Subscribed is of this Affirmant's proper Hand Writing and was by him Subscribed as a Witness to the Execution thereof (John Powell the other Witness Signing his Name as Witness at the Same time) And at the Same Time Came also to the above named Thomas Lincoln and Acknowledged the above Instrument of Writing to be his Act and Deed and desired the same might be recorded as such According to Law Witness my Hand and Seal the Day and Year aforesaid James Read (Seal) Recorded and this Record and the Original diligently compared and found to Agree exactly Word for Word and Figure for Figure the Twenty Sixth Day of October Anno Domini 1774.

The old Account Book of Abraham Lincoln shows that he ran a sawmill, which stood on the race running through the land of the brothers, Mordecai and Abraham Lincoln. The earliest reference in the account to the sawmill is found in the following entry made in the year 1758:

> Mordecai Lincoln to one half days sewing Jn exchange of Work
>
> £ s d
>
> Thomas Lincoln to Sawing of 60 foot 0 1 0

The mill account continues on into the seventies, showing that Abraham carried on a steady business at the mill.

In the land records the following references to the race and the sawmill are found:

"that nothing herein before mentioned expressed or contained shall in any wise prevent or hinder the said Mordecai Lincoln and Abraham Lincoln their Heirs Executors Administrators or Assigns or any of them from having or enjoying all the Liberties and Privileges to which they are respectively intitled to by Virtue of certain Articles of Agreement Dated the first Day of April Anno Domini one thousand seven hundred and fifty eight made between Abraham Lincoln George Henton, Mordecai Lincoln and Thomas Lincoln concerning a Water Saw Mill now erected and made on the Land of the said Mordecai Lincoln and Abraham Lincoln their Heirs and Assigns respectively are or shall be entitled to relative to the Water of the said Creek & Water Course aforesaid by Virtue of the Said recited Award] Said Mordecai Lincoln (Seal) Abraham Lincoln (Seal)"

* * * * * North five degrees East Eleven Perches to a Black Oak on the said Race thence on the same North four Degrees West Ten Perches to a White Oak Bush on Abraham Lincoln's Line thence by the same Abraham's Land South sev--enteen Degrees and a half West one hundred and nineteen Perches to an Ash Tree, on the West Bank of the Great Creek (being a Corner of the said Abraham and Thomas Lincoln's and William Tallman's Land) thence Crossing the Said Creek by Thomas Lincoln's Land . . . . . *

---

* This document is a Deed of Sale by William Tallman and Anne Tallman, his wife, to Jacob Bechtel Oct. 16, 1766.

The old Account Book of Abraham Lincoln, the posthumous son of Mordecai, the elder, of Exeter, is extant. It begins with 1756 and continues quite regularly until 1772 and after that with considerable gaps until 1779. The book affords an interesting glimpse into the daily occupations of the Lincolns, Boones, Hintons, Rogers and other families of Berks County before the Revolution. It is a rare document as an original source of Pennsylvania history. The MS. is 3 11/16 x 6 1/8 inches in size and contains 41 leaves. The book now belongs to Richard Lincoln, of Reading, Pennsylvania, who allowed the present writer to make use of it.

Abraham Lincoln was a man of importance in his community. The Commission Book for the years 1758-1783 shows that he was elected County Commissioner October, 1772, and served till 1779. He appears as Sub-Lieutenant in Berks County, March 21, 1777.

He was elected to the Assembly as follows:

October 28, 1782.
October 27, (?) 1783.
October 25, 1784.
October 24, 1785.

He served as assemblyman on the very important Committee of Grievances and was an important champion of the rights of the people in every measure that affected the delegation of the power of the people. This was particularly noticeable in constitu-

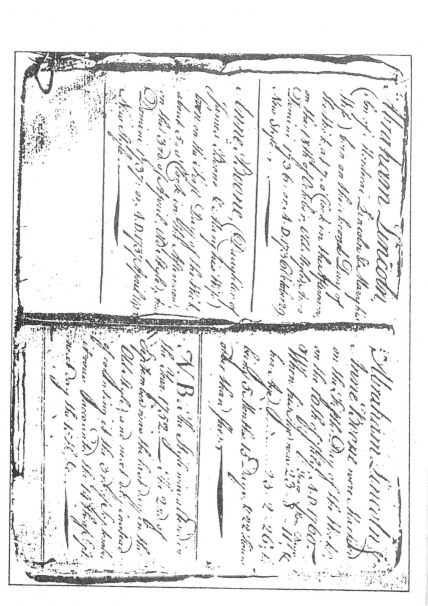

FIRST TWO PAGES OF THE OLD "LINCOLN RECORD."
(Original in the Possession of Harrison G. Lincoln, of Reading, Pa.)

tional discussions of 1785-6. Abraham Lincoln was chosen to make the address to Washington in Philadelphia after the close of the Revolution. He also took part in the Constitutional Convention of 1789-1790.*

As the Account Book shows, he was Supervisor of Roads and evidently entrusted with the repairs of the school house in 1771, showing probably that he was Chief School Commissioner. Abraham Lincoln died January 31, 1806, and was buried at Exeter. Ann, his wife and widow, died April 4, 1807, and was buried also at Exeter. The estates of both Abraham and Ann were settled by their children, as the accompanying photographic reproductions of the administrators' accounts with their signatures will show.

LINCOLN RECORD.

Abraham Lincoln (son of Mordecai Lincoln and Mary his Wife) born on the Second Day of the Week, at 7.. O Clock in the Afternoon on the 18th of October, Old Style, Anno Domini 1736: or, A. D. 1736 October 29, New Style.

Anna Boone (Daughter of James Boone and Mary his Wife) born on the First Day of the Week, about 5.. O'Clock in the Afternoon, on

---

* These facts relating to Abraham Lincoln's activity as a member of the Assembly are taken from a most interesting unpublished paper by Dr. A. H. Shearer, of Dartmouth College, who kindly allowed the present writer to make them public.

the 3rd of April, Old Style, Anno Domini 1737:
or, A. D. 1737 April 14th New Style.
Abraham Lincoln and Anna Boone were Married on the Fifth Day of the Week, on the
10th of July A. D. 1760 when his age was 23
Years 8 Mon. 11 Days and her Age was 23 " 2
" 26 " —he being 5 months 15 Days & 22 Hours
older than she.

N. B. The Style was altered in the Year
1752. The 2nd of September was the last day
in the Old Style; and next day instead of accounting it the 3rd of September it was accounted
the 14th of Sept. next day the 15th &c

Here follows the Times of the Births of the
Children of Abraham Lincoln & Anne Lincoln his
Wife, with the Differences of their Ages set down
likewise.

1st Mary Lincoln, (Daughter of Abraham Lincoln & Anne Lincoln) Born the 15th of September
Anno Domini 1761, on the Third Day of the Week,
about 10.. o'Clock at Night.

2nd Martha Lincoln, (Daughter of Abraham
Lincoln & Anne Lincoln) Born the 25th of January
Anno Domini 1763, on the Third Day of the Week,
about 10.. o'Clock in the Morning.

Martha being 1Y.. 4M.. 9D.. 12H. younger than
Mary.

3^d Mordecai Lincoln, junior, (son of Abraham
& Anne Lincoln) Born the 11th of January Anno
Domini 1765 on the Sixth Day of the Week about
15 Minutes after Seven in the Morning.

Mordecai being 1Y.. 11M.. 16D.. 21H.. 15 Min. younger than Martha.

4th James Lincoln (son of Abraham & Anne Lincoln Born the 5th of May Anno Domini 1767, on the Third Day of the Week, at or about 10.. o'Clock in the Morning.
James being 2Y.. 3M.. 24D.. 45m. younger than Mordecai.

5th Anna Lincoln, (Daughter of Abraham & Anne Lincoln Born the 19th of April Anno Domini 1769, on the 4th Day of the Week, at 7. o'Clock in the Morning.
Anna being 1Y.. 11M.. 13D.. 21H. younger than James.

6th Rachel Lincoln (Daughter of Abraham Lincoln & Anne Lincoln) Born the 24th of March A. D. 1771, on the First Day of the Week at 19 Minutes past 6.. o'Clock in the Morning.
Rachel being 1Y.. 11M.. 4D.. 23H.. younger than Anna.

7th Phebe Lincoln (Daughter of Abraham Lincoln and Anne Lincoln) Born in Anno Domini 1773 January 22^d. on the Sixth Day of the Week at 5 Minutes past 8.. o'Clock at Night.
Phebe being 1Y.. 9M.. 29D.: 13H.: 46m. younger than Rachel.

8th Anne Lincoln (Daughter of Abraham & Anne Lincoln) was born in Anno Domini 1774 October 19th on the Fourth Day of the Week, at 25 minutes past 11.. o'Clock in the Morning.
Anne being 1Y.: 8M.: 26D.: 15H.: 20m. younger than Phebe.

Rachel Lincoln (the 6th child of Abraham & Anne Lincoln) departed this Life on the Fourth Day of the Week, at 50 Minutes past 1 o'Clock in the Afternoon, and on the 19th day of July, A. D. 1775; aged 4Y.: 3M.: 25D.: 7H.: 31m. and was interred at Exeter the next Day.

9th Thomas Lincoln (son of Abraham & Anne Lincoln) was born on the Fourth Day of the Week at 10 Minutes past two in the Morning, and on the 12th Day of March A. D. 1777.

Thomas being 2Y.: 4.M.: 20D.: 14H.: 45m. younger than Anne.

10th John Lincoln (son of Abraham & Anne Lincoln) was born on the Fifth Day of the Week at ten Minutes past three in the Morning, and on the 21st Day of October A. D. 1779.

John being 2Y.: 7M.: 9D.: 1H. younger than Thomas.

Abraham Lincoln (son of Mordecai & Mary Lincoln) departed this Life, at his House in Exeter, on the 6th Day of the Week at 15 minutes past 7 in the Morning an^d on the 31st of January A. D. 1806 aged 69Y.: 3M.: 1D.: 7H.: 15M. and was interred at Exeter on the 2nd of February on the First Day of the Week.

Ann Lincoln (Widow of Abraham Lincoln) departed this Life in Exeter on the 7th day of the Week, at 10 minutes past 2 in the afternoon and on the 4th of April A. D. 1807 aged 69Y. 11M. 21D. 14H. 10m. and was interred at Exeter on the 6th of April on the 2nd day of the Week.

Julian Mayberry born the 5th Day of February A D 1780.

Mordecai Lincoln & Julian Mayberry were Married the 5th of May A. D. 1812 on the 3rd day of the Week at 8 O'Clock in the afternoon.

1. Rachel Lincoln (daughter of Mordecai & Julian Lincoln) was Born the 6th of May A. D. 1813 on the 5th day of the Week, at 6 o'clock in the Afternoon.

2. Ann Lincoln (Daughter of Mordecai & Julian Lincoln) born the 1st of August A. D. 1814 on the 2nd Day of the Week at 50 Minutes past 2 o Clock in the Morning.

Ann being 1Y.: 2M.: 24D.: 14H.: 50m. younger than Rachel.

3. Abraham M. Lincoln (son of Mordecai & Julian Lincoln) born the 1st of August A D 1814 on the 2nd Day of the Week, at 48 Minutes past 6 o Clock in the Morning.

Abraham being 3H.: 58m younger than Ann.

Ann Lincoln (Daughter of Mordecai & Julian Lincoln) departed this Life on the 4th of August 1814 on the 5th Day of the Week at 8 o Clock in the Morning Aged 3D.: 7H.: 12m.

Abraham Lincoln (son of Mordecai & Julian Lincoln) departed this Life on the 8th of August 1815 on the 3rd Day of the Week at 10 o.Clock at Night Aged 1Y.: 0M.: 7D.: 15H.: 12m.

4. Margaret Lincoln (Daughter of Mordecai & Julian Lincoln) born July 21 A D 1817, 40 minutes past 5 O Clock in the Morning And departed this Life 1817 on the 13th Day of August at 24 minutes past 3 o Clock in the Morning. Aged 22D.: 21H.: 44m.

5. Margaret Lincoln (Daughter of Mordecai & Julian Lincoln) born May 12th 1820 at o o Clock and 48 Minutes in the afternoon.

Mordecai Lincoln (Son of Abraham Lincoln & Anne his Wife) Departed this Life in Exeter Township the 12th day of September on the 5th day of the Week about 10 minutes before 6 o Clock in the afternoon A D 1822 Aged 57Y.: 8M.: 1D. When he had Lived with his Wife 10Y.: 3M. 7D.

Julian Lincoln Widow of Mordecai Lincoln Departed this life in Allentown Lehigh Co. the 6th Day of March on the 7th day of the Week about 12 o Clock noon A D 1858 Aged 78 Y.: 1M.: 1D.

Margaret Lincoln & Bartholomew Barto were Married Dec 7th 1841 Her Age being 21Y.: 8M.: 7D.

Alice Dehaven daughter of Abraham Dehaven from Lancaster Co. and wife of Thomas Lincoln was born June 25th 1770. She departed this Life Dec 29th 1836 Aged 66 Y. 6M. 3D.

Thomas Lincoln departed this life Dec 27th 1863 Aged 86Y. 9M. 15D.

Martha Lincoln daughter of Thomas & Allice Lincoln departed this Life Oct. 12th 1858 at 9 o clock in the morning Aged 46Y.: 10M.: 20D. (called also Martha Kaub) Grave is 6th in 5th row at Exeter Meeting.

John D Lincoln son of Thomas & Alice Lincoln was born Jan 1 1815 on the 1st day of the Week.

[Book is here defaced, but it appears to be a record of a 2nd Marriage of Thomas Lincoln to

Hannah E——, who was born the 7th of March, 1827, near Douglassville—Harrison P. Lincoln.] John Lincoln son of Abraham Lincoln, departed this life on the 4th Day of April 1864 Aged 84Y. 5M. 21D.

James Lincoln son of Abraham Lincoln died in Carnarven Twp. Berks Co. in Morgantown 3rd day of Week between 8 & 9 o'Clock in the morning A D 1860 Aged 93 Y. 7M. 6D. Interred at Morgantown 13th.

David J. Lincoln died April 10th 1886 at Birdsborough Aged 70 years.

Children of John D. & Sarah Lincoln.

1 Ametia Born March 28 1838
2 Alfred   "   Apr 21 1839
3 Harrison H. Born July 28 1840
4 Elizabeth   "   Nov 20 1841
5 John   "   Mar 7 1843 Died July 19 1876
6 Richard Born Dec 5th 1844
7 Martha   "   "   12th 1846
8 Ann (or Anna) Born Feb 16th 1849
9 Sarah   "   May 24th 1851
10 Mary   "   Apr 24th 1852
11 Oscar   "   Feb 16 1855 Died Apr 25th 1857

[Book is here defaced but record appears to read that John D Lincoln married Sarah Solbert or Gilbert on Jan 2th 1837 and that he died Jan 27 1868—Harrison P. Lincoln]*

---

* The copy made by Harrison P. Lincoln, now found in the Historical Society of Pennsylvania, has been used in connection with the original manuscript Lincoln Record.

CHAPTER VI.

JOHN LINCOLN OR "VIRGINIA JOHN," SON OF MORDECAI OF EXETER.

It is with John Lincoln, the third son of Mordecai Lincoln, the elder, of Exeter, that the Lincoln line continues its migration from Pennsylvania into Virginia, the Great Valley and the Middle West. It has been possible to trace the track of this migration in the land records and other documents.

According to the will of his father, Mordecai Lincoln, the elder, of Exeter, John Lincoln received his share of the estate his father's land in New Jersey. So whatever land he possessed in Pennsylvania had to be acquired by purchase in some form. The earliest mention of John Lincoln in the land records of Pennsylvania is found in proprietary grant dated June 28, 1746, and runs as follows:

THOMAS PENN & RICHARD PENN

Esquires true and absolute Proprietaries and Governors in Chief of the Province of Pennsylvania and Counties of Newcastle Kent & Sussex upon Delaware To all unto whom these Presents shall come Greeting:

WHEREAS in Pursuance of a Warrant dated the Twenty eighth Day of Iune one thousand seven hundred and forty six there was surveyed unto Iohn Lloyd A certain Tract of Land situate in

Union Street in the County of Berks Beginning
at a marked black Oak Thence by vacant Land
South West seventy nine Perches to a Post South
East one hundred and eight Perches to a Chestnut Oak and North East seventy nine Perches
to a Post Thence by John Lloyd's other Land
North West one hundred and eight Perches to
the Place of Beginning Containing Fifty Acres
and forty nine Perches and Allowance of Six
Acres Pr Cent for Roads & Highways As in and
by the said Warrant and Survey remaining in the
Surveyor Generals Office & from thence Certified
into our Secretaries Office more fully appears and
Whereas the said John Lloyd in and by his Deed
or Articles of Agreement dated the ninth day of
October one thousand seven hundred and forty
six did grant bargain & sell all his Right to the
said Warrant Land & Improvements with the Appurtenances unto John Lincoln then of Caernarvon Township Yeoman his Heirs & Assigns for
ever As by the said Deed now produced appears
Now at the Instance and Request of the said
John Lincoln that we would be pleased to grant
him a Confirmation of the same know Ye that in
Consideration of the sum of Three Pounds fifteen
Shillings and eleven Pence lawful Money of Pennsylvania to our Use paid by the said John Lincoln (The Receipt whereof we hereby acknowledge and thereof do acquit and for ever Discharge the said John Lincoln his Heirs and Assigns by the Presents) and of the yearly Quitrent
hereinafter mentioned and reserved We have
given granted released and confirmed and by

these Presents do give grant release and confirm
unto the said John Lincoln his Heirs and Assigns the said Fifty Acres & forty-nine Perches
of Land as the same are now set forth bounded
and limited as aforesaid With all Mines Minerals
Quarries Meadows Marshes Savannahs Swamps
Cripples Woods Underwoods Timber and Trees
Ways Waters Watercourses Liberties Profits
Commodities Advantages Hereditaments & Appurtenances whatsoever thereunto belonging or
in any wise appurtaining and lying within the
Bounds & Limits aforesaid [Three full & clear
fifth Parts of all Royal Mines free from all De-
ductions and Reprizals for digging & refining
the same and also one fifth Part of the Ore of
all other Mines delivered at the Pitsmouth only
excepted and hereby reserved] and also free
Leave Right and Liberty to and for the said
John Lincoln his Heirs and Assigns to Hawk
Hunt Fish & Fowl in & upon the hereby granted
Land and Premises or upon any Part thereof To
HAVE AND TO HOLD the said fifty Acres and forty
nine Perches of Land & Premises hereby
granted (except as before excepted) with their
Appurtenances unto the said John Lincoln his
Heirs and Assigns To the only Use & Behoof of
the said John Lincoln his Heirs and Assigns for
ever To BE HOLDEN of us our Heirs & Succes-
sors Proprietaries of Pennsylvania as of our
Manor of Ruscombe in the County of Berks
aforesaid in free & common Soccage by Fealty
only in Lieu of all other Services yielding and
Paying therefore yearly unto us our Heirs and

Successors at the Town of Reading in the said
County at or upon the first day of March in every
year one half Penny Sterling for every Acre of
the same Or Value thereof in Coin Current account according as the Exchange shall then
be between our said Province and the City
of London to such Person or Persons as shall
from Time to Time be appointed to receive the
same And in Case of Nonpayment thereof within
ninety Days next after the same shall become due
That then it shall and may be lawful for us our
Heirs and Successors our and their Receiver or
Receivers into and upon the hereby granted Land
& Premises to Reenter & the same to hold
and possess until the said Quitrent and all ar-
rears thereof Together with the Charges accruing
by means of such Nonpayment & Reentry be fully
paid and discharged WITNESS John Penn Esquire
Lieutenant Governor of the said Province Who by
Virtue of certain Powers & Authorities to him for
this Purpose inter alia, granted by the said Proprietaries hath hereunto set his Hand and caused
the Great Seal of the said Province to be hereunto affixed at Philadelphia this seventh day of
Iune in the year of our Lord one thousand seven
hundred and sixty five The Fifth Year of the
Reign of King George the Third over Great Britain &c and the Forty seventh year of the said
Proprietaries Government Iohn Penn (L. S.) Recorded the 10th day of Iune, 1765.

A very important deed, dated November 8, 1748,

in which John Lincoln conveys his land in New Jersey to William Dye, gives us much valuable information, showing that he was the son of Mordecai, the elder, of Exeter, and a weaver by trade, then living in Caenarvon, Lancaster County, Pennsylvania:

THIS INDENTURE made the eighth day of November in the twentyeth second year of the Reigne of our Soveraigne Lord George the Second of Great Brittain france and Ireland King Defender of the faith &c in the Year of Our Lord one thousand seven hundred and forty eight Between John Lincon of the Township Carnarvin in the County of Lancaster and Province of Penselvania weaver the son and Heir of Mordecai Lincon deceased of the one part and William Dye of the County of Middlesex yeoman of the other Part Witnesseth that the said John Lincon for and in Consideration of the Sum of Two hundred pounds current money of New Jersey at eight shillings p ounce to me in hand paid by him the said William Dye the receipt whereof he the said John Lincon doth hereby acknowledge and himself to be therewith satisfied contented & paid and thereof and of and from every part and parsal thereof doth fully clearly and absolutely acquit exonerate and discharge him the said William Dye his Heirs Executors Administrators and assigns for ever Hath Granted bargained Sold aliened Convaid and Confirmed unto him the said William Dye and to his Heirs and assigns forever All that Tract of Land scituate lying and being in

the said County of Middlesex Beginning where
the Land formerly Walter Benthals crosses
Crarnberry brook from thence along said Benthals line towards the Post Road to the Land formerly Robert Burnets And from thence along
said Burnets line in breadth so far that a parallel
line to the foresaid line of Benthels from the said
Burnets line to said Cranberry brook do contain
three hundred acres thence along the course of
said Benthals line to Cranberry brook and from
thence down the Brook to where it began Bounded Westerly by the Land formerly said Benthals
Northerly by Land formerly Robert Burnets
Easterly by Land formerly belonging to Herricon
and Southerly by Cranberry brook with all and
all manner of Houses Building [s] Mines Minerals
and Appurtenances and previliges .whatsoever of
him the said John Lincon as well in Law as in
Equity of in or unto the said three hundred acres
of Land with the Reversion and Reversions Remainders of the Same To Have and to Hold the
aforesaid Three hundred acres of Land with all
the bargained Premises with the Appurtenances
unto him the said William Dye his Heirs and
assigns for ever to the only proper use benefit
and behoof of him the said William Dye his
Heirs and assigns And he the said John Lincon
for himself his Heirs Executors and administrators by these Presents in manner following viz
That he the said John Lincon at the time of the
Sealing & Delivering hereof hath in himself
good Right full Power and lawful Authority to

Grant bargain Sell Convey the said Three hundred acres of Land unto the said William Dye in manner as aforesaid and that the same is and shall continue free and clear from all incumbrances whatsoever and will Warrant secure and Defend the said William Dye his Heirs and assigns for ever In Witness Whereof I have hereunto Set my hand and Seal the day and year abovesaid. John Lincon (L: S) Signed Sealed and Delivered in Presence of us John Brainerd, Ebenezer Hayward Memorandum that on the 24th day of May 1750 John Lincon party to the within written Instrument appeared before me Andrew Johnson one of His Majesty's Council for the Province of New Jersey and acknowledged that he executed the same as his voluntary act and Deed of the therein mentioned And^w Johnson

The name of John Lincoln appears in the early tax lists of Berks County, Pennsylvania, as the following assessments will show:

		£	£	s.	d.	Township
1754	John Lincorn	38		9	6	Union
1758	John Lincoln	6		1	6	Amity
1758	John Lincoln					
	Nov 29 1758	4		6		Amity
	(Special Assessment)					
1758	John Lincoln	10		15		Union
1759	Linckcoln John	10		15		Union
1759	Lincoln John		1			Amity
	(Single Man)					
1759	Lincoln John	6		9		Amity

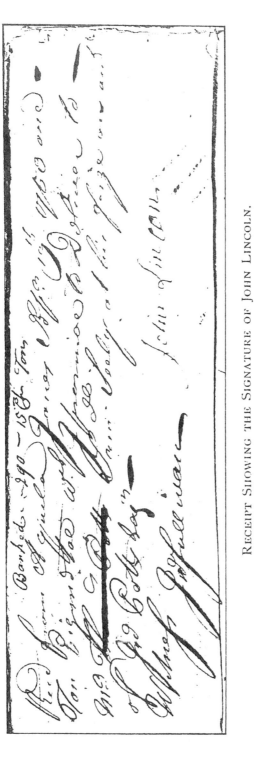

RECEIPT SHOWING THE SIGNATURE OF JOHN LINCOLN.

(Original is in the Collection of Former Governor S. W. Pennypacker.)

1760	Lincoln, John	12			Union
1760	Lincoln [John?]	8	12		Amity
1760	Lincoln [John?]	13	19	6	Union
1761	Lincoln Jnº.	12	3		
	[married men]				
1762	Lincoln John	16	4		Amity
1762	Lincoln John	8	12		Amity
1763	Lincoln John	16	4		Amity
1763	Lincoln John	13	19	6	Amity
1764	Lincoln John	17	4	3	Amity
1765	Lincoln John	13	9	6	Amity

Although John Lincoln is mentioned in the land papers as weaver by trade, he had other forms of occupation. The following receipt, dated June 10, 1754, shows that he was engaged in the business of hauling, at least at times:

Recd from Aquila Jones Sepr. 19th 1753 one Ton Pigmetal wch J promice to Deliver to Mr. Samll Seely at his forge on acct of Jno Potts Esqr

Witness

Jnº Sullivan   John Lincon

There are a number of records of land transactions by John Lincoln in the land papers of Berks County, as the following will show:

Grantee John Lincoln, June 13, 1748, Grantor John Loyd and wife, Robeson, Lanc. Co., book 8, page 400.

Grantor John Lincoln, May 17, 1763, Grantee Jacob
Redcay, Robeson, book 8, page 402.
Grantee John Lincoln, June 14, 1763, Grantor John Camp-
bell, Amity, book 4, page 319.
Grantor John Lincoln, May 20, 1765, Grantee Henry Leer,
Amity, book 4, page 323.
Grantee John Lincoln, May 27, 1765, Grantors William
Boone, Jeremiah Boone, book 4, page 321.
Grantor John Lincoln, June 13, 1765, Grantee Jacob
Redcay, Union, book 8, page 404.

According to these deeds, John Lincoln and Rebecca, his wife, disposed of their important tracts of
land between 1763 and 1765, as follows:

1. They sold to Jacob Redcay, May 17, 1763, 120
acres of the land granted to John Lincoln by the Proprietary authority June 13, 1748, for the sum of
300 pounds.

2. They sold to Henry Lear, May 20, 1765, one
tract of 125 acres and another of 36 acres for 4
pounds per acre.

3. They sold to the aforesaid Jacob Redcay, June
13, 1765, 50 acres and 49 perches for the sum of
120 pounds.

Thus they sold altogether 331 acres and 49 perches
of land for the sum of 794 pounds in all, during
these two years.

Meanwhile John Lincoln had bought of John
Campbell, of Amity township, 36 acres of land for
100 pounds, and of William and Jeremiah Boone,
sons and executors of George Boone, of Exeter, 125

acres for the sum of 160 pounds. Thus he had invested during those two years 260 pounds in land and realized 794 pounds from sales of land, leaving a net cash balance of 534 pounds.

It is significant that the name of John Lincoln disappears from the Berks County records about 1765. The question naturally arises: What became of him? The answer to this question is easily found in the land records of Virginia. An original deed found in the Recorder's Office of Staunton, Virginia, and dated June 21, 1768, furnishes the desired information:

> THIS INDENTURE made the twenty first day of June in the year of our Lord one thousand seven hundred and sixty eight BETWEEN Zachariah and Lydia Moses (Mases?) and Mary McKoy [McKay?] their wifes [sic] Robert and James McKoy [McKay?] of the County of Fredrick and Colony of Virginia of the one part and John Lincon of the County of augusta and Colony aforesaid of the other part—witnesseth that the said Zachariah and Lydia Moses and Mary McKay for and in consideration of the sum of five shillings current money of Virginia unto them in hand paid by the said John Lincon at or before the sealing and Delivery of these Presents the Receipt whereof is hereby acknowledged hath granted Bargained and sold and by these Presents doth grant bargain and sell unto the said John Lincon a tract of Land containing six hundred acres more or Less lying and being in the County of Augusta

on Linwils Creek being a Parcel of twelve hundred acres granted by Patent to McCoy Duff
Green and Hite by Patent Bearing date the twen-
-ty six day of March 1739 and by them convey to
Robert McKay by Deeds of Lease and Release
dated the nineteenth and 20th days of June
MDCC46 and recorded in the County Court of
Augusta and by the said Robert McKay &c and
devised to the aforesaid Zachariah McKay and
Lydia Moses and Mary McKay their wifes [sic]
by his Last will and Testament Bearing Date the
day of   MDCC   duely Proved and
Recorded in the County Court of Augusta the
said tract being bounded as followeth to wit BE-
GINNING at a Black oak the south side of a ridge
corner to Tunis Vanpelt Land in original line Nº.
54º. W. 662 Poles containuing that *cost* to the
Origenial [sic] Line thence Nº. 37º degs. Et. 108
poles to Bomans Line in the Original line
thence Sº. 26º W. 80 Poles to an off set in the
Original Line Running thence with the said Line
Sº. 39º W. 108 Poles to the Place of BEGINNING
and all houses Orchards ways Waters Watercourses profits commodities hereditaments and
appurtenances whatsoever to the said Premises
hereby granted or any part thereof belonging or
in anywise appertaining and the Reversion and
Reversions Remainder and Remainders rents Issues and Profits thereof TO have and to hold the
said six hundred acres more or Less of Land and
all and singular other the Premises is hereby
granted with the appurtenances unto the said John

Lincon and his Executors and administrators and assigns from the day before the date hereof for and During the full term and time of one whole year from thence next ensuing fully to be complete and ended YIELDING and Paying therefore the rent of one pepper   on Lady day next if the same shall be Lawfully Demanded to the Intent and purpose that by Virtue of these Presents and of the statute for transferring uses into Possession the said John Lincon may be in actual Possession of the Premises and to be thereby enabled to accept and take a grant and Release of the Reversion and Inheritance thereof to him and his heirs IN WITNESS whereof the said Zachariah and Lydia Moses and Mary McCoy their wifes *Roberd* and James McCoy hath *hath* hereunto set their hands and seals the day and year first above written.

Zachariah McKay.	(L. S.)
Moses McKay.	(L. S.)
Robert McKay.	(L. S.)
James McKay	(L. S.)

Sealed and Delivered
in the Presence of
Michael Waren.
          his
John [8] Jackson.
       mark
John Poage.

At a Court held for Augusta County August the 16th, 1768.

This Lease from Zachariah McKay Robert Mc-

Kay Moses McKay and James McKay to John
Lincon was Proved by the oaths of the Witnesses
thereto and Ordered to be Recorded.

Test John Madison

Copied from Deed Book No. 15 Page 50
Clerk's Office of the Circuit Court for Augusta
County, Virginia.

Harry Burnett, Clerk.

[The record shows that the sum of £250 was
paid. The forms of the name 'McKay' and 'Mc-
Koy' (as written at the beginning of the deed)
are, of course, identical.]

It is clear from the deed that John Lincoln had
migrated to Virginia between the years 1765 and
1768. The fact that the signatures of John Lincoln
and the mark of Rebecca Lincoln, his wife, are
identical in the land documents of Berks County,
Pennsylvania and in those of Augusta County, Virginia, leaves no possible doubt of the identity of the
persons themselves. The signature of John Lincoln
in the Virginia deed of 1773 is very poor, but nevertheless legible. By an omission easily explained, the
usual mark or sign of Rebecca's "mark" was not
affixed to the document here reproduced, but that her
signature was certified to is indicated in the recorded deed. It was our good fortune to find a particularly good specimen of John Lincoln's signature
in an old receipt found in the collections of Ex-Gov-
ernor Pennypacker, who generously allowed it to be
reproduced in this work. In the light of these docu-

DEED OF JOHN AND REBECCA LINCOLN TO ISAAC LINCOLN, CONVEYING
LAND ON LINVILLE'S CREEK IN 1773.

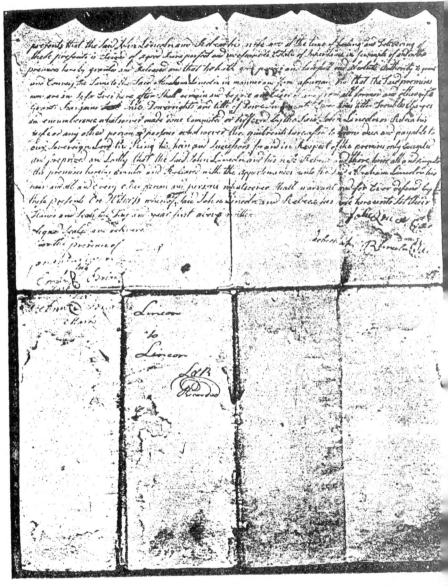

DEED OF JOHN AND REBECCA LINCOLN TO ISAAC LINCOLN, CONVEYIN[G] LAND ON LINVILLE'S CREEK IN 1773.

ments, the current statement that John Lincoln went to Virginia to settle about 1750, at the time when Daniel Boone left Berks County, Pennsylvania, for the South, must be considered incorrect. Nevertheless, it was in the track of Daniel Boone that John Lincoln found his way to Virginia and the tradition that Daniel Boone stopped for a time on Linvill's Creek in Augusta (now Rockingham) County, Virginia, doubtless reflects important history in connection with the migration from Pennsylvania to Virginia. Moreover, the intimate relations of the Lincolns and the Boones in Berks County, Pennsylvania, give us the motive for such migration at this time.

The land records of Virginia show also how John Lincoln distributed his land in Augusta County to his sons. In the following deed, dated August 12, 1773, he conveys to his son, Isaac Lincoln, 215 acres of his 600 acre purchase of 1768, as the text of the document will show:

> THIS INDENTURE made the Twelfth day of August in the year of our Lord one thousand seven hundred and Seventy three Between John Lincoln and Rebeca his wife of Augusta County & Colony of Virginia of the one part and Isaac Lincoln of the County and Colony aforesaid of the other Part Witnesseth that for and in consideration of the sum of Twenty Pounds Current mony of Virginia to the said John Lincoln in hand Paid by the said Isaac Lincoln at or before the

Sealing & delivering of these Presents the receipt
he doth hereby Acknowledge & thereof doth release acquit and Discharge the said Isaac Lincoln
his Executors & Administrators by these Presents
that the said John Lincoln Hath Granted Bargained sold Aliened released and Confirmed &
by these Presents doth Grant Bargain Sell Alien
release & Confirm unto the sd. Isaac Lincoln (in
his Actuall Possession now being by virtue of a
Bargain and Sale to him thereof made by the
said John Lincoln & Rebecca his wife for one
whole year by Indenture bearing date the day
next before the day of the date of these Presents
and by force of the Statute for Transfering uses
into Possession/ and his heirs one Certain Tract
or Parcel of Land Containing 215 acres Lying
and being in the County of Augusta on Lenvels
Creek being Part of Twelve Hundred acres
Granted to McKay Duff Green and Hite by Pat-
tent Bearing date the 26th. day of March 1739
and was by them Conveyed to Robert McKay by
deeds of Lease and Release Bearing date the 19th.
and 20th. days of June 1746 & recorded in the
County Court of Augusta & was by the said Robert McKay Devised to Zachariah McKay Mosses
McKay Robert McKay and James McKay by his
Last will and Testament dated the 7th. day of
Octobed 1746 and recorded in the County Court
of Augusta and Six hundred Acres Part of the
Twelve hundred acres was Conveyed by the said
Zachariah McKay and Lydia his wife Mosses
McKay and Mary his wife Robert McKay and

James McKay unto the [said] John Lincoln by deeds of Lease and release bearing date the 21st. and 22nd., days of June, 1768 and recorded in the County Court of Augusta and Bounded as followeth, to wit:—Beginning at a Black and white oake Saplings on the old line Corner to his Brother Abrahams Land & thence south 31 degrees west 16 poles to 2 white oake Saplins thence south 54 degrees east 240 Poles to the Creek a Marked walnutt a Corner to the said Abrahams Land north 86 degrees east 13 poles Crossing the Creek to 2 Locusts thence North 39 degrees 8 poles to a Black and white oak Saplins south 62 degrees East 360 Poles to a Black oak Saplin on the old Line north 60 degrees east 5 poles to 2 white oaks an old Corner thence north 22 degrees east & 80 poles to 2 white oaks thence north 65½ degrees west 360 poles to the Creek & the same Course 252 poles to the Beginning and all houses Buildings Orchards ways water water Courses Profits Commodities Hereditaments and Appurtenances whatsoever to the said Premises hereby Granted or and Part thereof Belonging or in any wise appertaining and the reversion and reversions Remainder and Remainders Rents Issues & Profits thereof and also all the estate right title Interest use Trust Property Claim and demand and whatsoever of them the said John Lincoln and Rebeca his wife of in and to the said Premises and all deeds Evidences & writings touching or in any wise Concerning the same To have and To hold the Lands hereby Con-

veyed and all and Singular other the Premises
hereby Granted & released and every Part and
Parcel thereof with their and every of their Appurtenances unto the said Isaac Lincoln his heirs
and Assigns forever To the only proper use and
Behoof of him the said Isaac Lincoln his heirs
and Assigns forever and the said John Lincoln
and Rebeca his wife for themselves there heirs
Executors and Administrators doth Covenant
Promise & Grant to and with the said Isaac Lincoln his heirs and Assigns by these Presents that
the said John Lincoln and Rebeca his wife now
at The time of Sealing and Delivering of these
Presents is Seized of a good sure Perfect and
Indefeasible estate of Inheritance in fee Simple
of and in the Premises hereby Granted and released and that they have Good Power and Lawful and Absolute Authority to Grant and Convey
the same to the said Isaac Lincoln in Manner and
form aforesaid and that the said Premises now
are and so forever hereafter shall remain and be
free and Clear of and from all former and other
Gifts Grants Bargains sales Dower rights and
title of dower Judgments Executions Titles
Troubles Charges and Encumbrances whatsoever
made done Committed or suffered by the said
John Lincoln & Rebeca his wife or any other Person or Persons whaostever [sic] (the Quit Rents
hereafter to Grow due and Payable to our Sovereign Lord the king his heirs and Successors for
and in Respect of the Premises only excepted and
Foreprized) AND LASTLY that the said John Lin-

coln & Rebeca his Wife and there heirs all and Singular the Premises hereby Granted & Released with the Appurtenances unto the said Isaac Lincoln his heirs and Assigns against them the said John Lincoln and Rebeca his Wife and their heirs & all and every other Person & Persons whatsoever shall warrant and forever defend by these Presents In witness whereof the said John Lincoln and Rebeca his wife have hereunto set their hands and Seals the day and year first Written.

John Lincoln,   (L. S.)

her
Rebeckah R. Lincoln, (L. S.)
mark

Signed Sealed & Delivered—
In the Presence of—
Josiah Davison
    his
Cornelius [B] Briant
    mark
  her
Ann (.) Briant.
  mark

At a Court held for Augusta County August the 17th., 1773.

This Release for Land from John Lincoln and Rebecah his wife to Isaac Lincoln was Proved by the Oaths of the witnesses thereto and Ordered to be Recorded.

Teste John Madison

A copy Teste: Harry Burnett, Clerk.

CHAPTER VII.

ABRAHAM LINCOLN OF VIRGINIA AND KENTUCKY.

Turning now to John Lincoln's son, Abraham, the grandfather of President Lincoln, we find him also carrying on extensive land transactions in Augusta County, Virginia, and later in Kentucky. In addition to his land mentioned in the deed to Isaac Lincoln, his brother, given above, he buys additional land. In a deed dated September 6, 1779, he buys of Holten Munsey and Else, his wife, a tract of 52 acres of land for 500 pounds:

> This Indenture Made the sixth day of September in the year of our Lord one thousand and Seven Hundred and Seventy Nine Between Holten Muncey and Eles [Else?] his Wife of the County of Rockingham and the State of Virginia of the one part and Abraham Lincoln of the County Afore Said and the State of Virginia of the Other Part WITNESSETH that for and in Consideration of the sum of five Hundred Pounds Current Money of Virginia in hand Paid to the said Holten Muncey and his Wife by the said Abraham Lincoln at Or before the Sealing and Delivery of these Presents the Receipt whereof they Doth hereby Acknowledge and thereof doth Release Acquit and discharge the Said Abraham Lincoln his heirs and assigns by these presents he the Said Holten Muncey hath granted Bargined Sold Aliened and Confirmed and by these Presents doth grant Bargain Sell Alien and Confirme rent

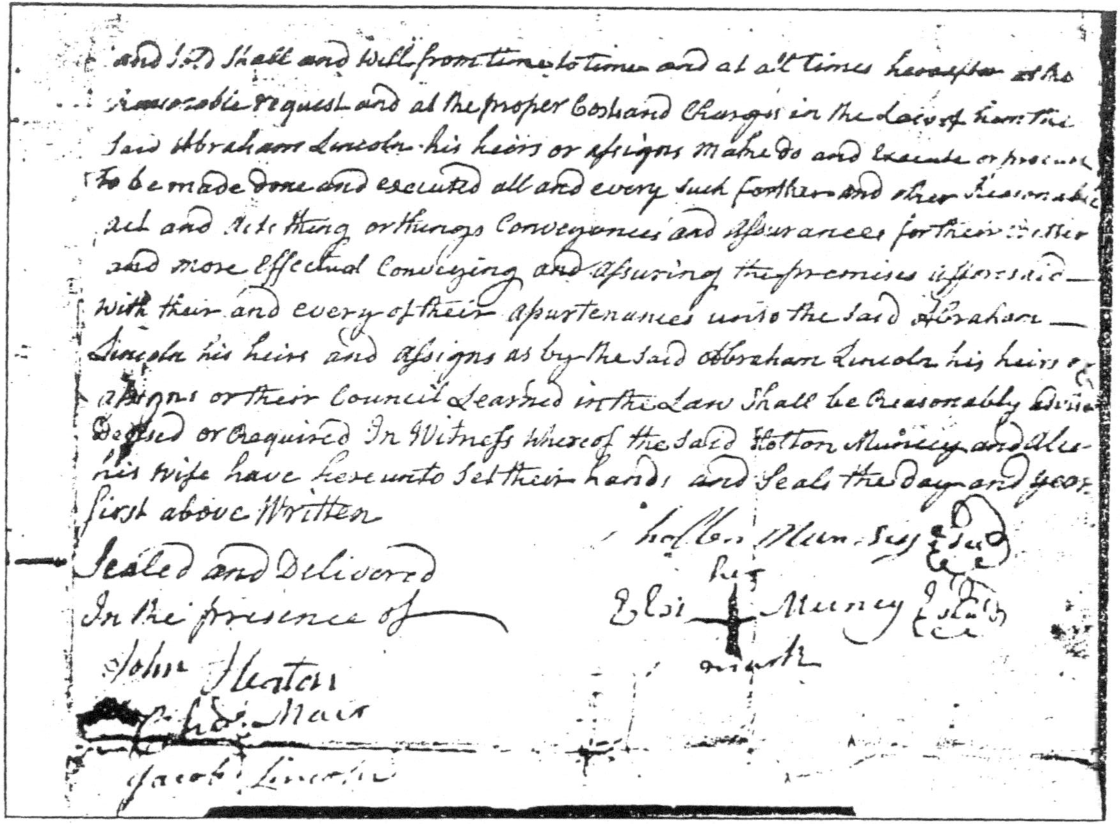

[unto?] the said Abraham Lincoln his heirs and Assigns for Ever one Sertain tract or Parsel of land Containing fifty two Acres lying and being on Linvils Creek in the County of Rockingham and Bounded as followeth Viz Begining at a white Oak on Said Lincolns Line thence Crossing the tract S. 42 W. 104 poles to A white Oak thence S. E. 34 Poles to A wite [sic] Oak tree and two Saplins thence N. 76 E. 76 Poales to a Locast Steak thence S. 52 E. 41 Poales to a Locast stake thence North 36 E 55 Poales to 2 Small hickeries thence with the old Line to the Beginning Corner Containing fifty two Accres Be the Same More or Less Being formerly Convaid to the Said Holten Muncey by Tunis Vanpelt and Thomas Briant by Deeds of Leas and Releas dated————— the said tract of Land being Part of A larger Tract of Seven thousand and Nine Acres Granted to Jost Hite Robert McCoy Robert Green and William Duff By Patent Bearing Date the twenty Six day of March 1739 and all houses Buildings orchards Ways waters water Corses profits Commodities Hereditaments and Appurtenance Whatsoever to the Said Premises hereby Granted or Any Part Thereof Belonging to or in Any Wise Apertaining and the Reversion and Reversions Remainder and Remainders Rents Issues and Profits there of and also all the Estate Right Title Use Trust Profit or Claim or demand Whatsoever of him the Said Holten Muncey of In and to the Said Premises and all Deeds Evidences and Writings Touching or in Any Wise Concerning the same to have and to hold the Lands hereby Conveyed and all and Singular other the prem-

ises hereby bargained and Sold and every part
and parcel thereof with their and every part of
their appurtenances unto the said Abraham Lincoln his heirs and assigns forever to the only
proper use and Behoof of him the said Abraham
Lincoln & of his heirs and assigns forever and
the said Holton Muncey and Alce [=Elsi] his
wife for themselves their heirs and assigns by
these presents that Holton Muncey [and] Alce his
wife now at the Time of Sealing and Delivering of
these presents is Seized of a good Sure perfect and
Indefeasable Estate of Inheritance in Fee simple
of and in the said premises hereby granted and
that they have good power Lawfull and absolute
Right and Authority to grant and Convey the
same to the said Abraham Lincoln in manner
and form aforesaid and that the premises now
are & so forever hereafter shall Remain and be
free and Clear of and from all others and former
gifts grants Bargains Sales Dower Right and
Title of Dower—Judgments Executions Titles
Troubles Charges and Incumbrances Whatsoever
Made Done Committed or Suffered by the Said
Holton Muncey or Alce his Wife or any other
person or persons Whatsoever (The Assessment
hereafter to grow Due and payable to the Collec-
tor for the time being for the use of the Commonwealth of Virginia) for and in Respect of the
premises only Excepted and and [sic] foreprized
and the said Holton Muncey and Alce his wife and
their heirs and all and Singular the premises hereby granted with their appurtenances unto the said
Abraham Lincoln his heirs and assigns against
them the said Holton Muncey and Alce his Wife

and their heirs and all and every other person or persons Whatsoever Shall and Will Warrant and forever defend by these presents and Lastly that the said Holton Muncey and Alce his Wife and their heirs and every other person or persons and their heirs anything Having and Claiming in the premises herein before Mentioned or Intended to be hereby Bargained and sold shall and Will from time to time and at all times hereafter at the Reasonable request and at the proper Costs and Charges in the Law of him the Said Abraham Lincoln his heirs or assigns make do and execute or procure to be made done and executed all and every such farther and other Reasonable Act and Acts thing or things conveyances assurances for their Better and more effectual conveying and assuring the premises afforesaid with their and every of their apurtenances unto the said Abraham Lincoln his heirs and assigns as by the said Abraham Lincoln his heirs or assigns or their Council Learned in the Law shall be Reasonably advised Devised or Required. In Witness whereof the said Holton Muncey and Alce his Wife have herewith set their hands and Seals the day and year first above Written.

holten Munsey   (Seal)

her

Elsi [X] Muncy   (Seal)

mark

Sealed and Delivered
In the presence of
John Heaton
Chas Mair
Jacob Lincoln

At a court held for Rockingham County the 22
Day of November 1779 This Deed of Bargain &
Sale for Holton Muncy to Abraham Lincoln was
proved by the Oaths of the witnesses thereto &
ordered to be recorded

Test. Pet'. Hog C. R. c.
Monsey
to
Lincoln No & Sale 91
Record^d & Exam^d
? Ervin C. R. C.

Recorded in Burnt Records
Deed Book No. O page 53
C. H. Brunk D. C.

[The correct form of the name in this deed
seems to be 'Holten' although toward the end of
the deed it is written 'Holton.' It will be noted
too that the last name is written 'Munsey' 'Muncey,' 'Muncy.' In like manner the wife's name
is written 'Eles,' 'Alce,' and 'Elsi' (in the signature).]

The next year, 1780, we find a most important
land transaction of this Abraham Lincoln, the son
of "Virginia John," recorded in a deed dated February 18, 1780. By this document Abraham Lincoln and his wife, "Batseb" (Bethsheba), sell to
Michael Shanks and John Ruef, also of the same
county (now Rockingham), 250 acres (part of the
original purchase of John Lincoln), for the sum of
5000 pounds. This price seems very high, but it

Old Lincoln House on Linville's Creek, Rockingham County, Virginia.

must be remembered that Abraham Lincoln paid half that price (10 pounds per acre) for the 52 acres bought the year before. The text of the deed follows:

THIS INDENTURE made the Eighteenth day of Feberuary [sic] in the Year of our Lord one thousand Seven Hundred and Eighty Between Abraham Lincolen of the County of Rockingham and State of Virginia and Bersheba [Bethsheba? not Barbara as the deed book has it] his wife of the one part and Michel shanks and John Reuf [Ruef] of the county and State aforesaid of the other Part Witnesseth that for and in consideration of the sume of five Thousand Poundes Current money of Virginia in hand paid unto the said Ab^m Lincolen By the Said Michel shanks at or Before the sealing and Delivery of these presents the Receipt whereof they doth hereby acknowledge and and thereof doth Release aquit and Discharge the Said Michal [sic] shanks his Heirs and assigns by these presents he the said Ab^m Lincolen hath Granted Bargained Sold Alien'd and Confirmed and by these presents doth grant Bargain sell alien and Confirm unto the said Michal shanks and their heirs and assigns for ever one Certain Tract of Land Containing two hundred and fifty acres Being a part of twele [twelve] hundred acres Granted to Mc-Kay Duff Green and Hite By patent bearing Date twenty six dayes [sic] March 1739 and by them Convey'd to Robert McKay by Deeds of Lease and Release bearing date the nineteenth and twenty Dayes of June 1746 and by the Said Robert McKay Devised to the afor said Zachariah mcKay Moses McKay Robert McKay and the aforsaid McKayes convey to John Lincolen six hundred acres of the forsaid Land by Deed of Lease and Realse [sic?] bearing Date the twenty Second day of June 1768 and John Lincolen Conveyed apart of this within mentioned two hundred and fifty acres to Abraham Lincolen and Tunis Vanpelt Thos Bryan and Holten Muncey Conveyed the Rest the said Land to abrm Lincolen Lying and being on the North side of Linvils Creek Beginning at a Locust Stake and walnut stump on the North side of Linvils Creek thence along the old Line South thirty seven Degrees West Seventy Eight Poles to a black oak corner to Tunis Vanpelt North fifty five and a half Degrees West one hundred and twenty four poles to white oak one [sic] said line: south forty two Degrees West one hundred & four Poles to a whit oak South East thirty Poles to white oak and two Sapplins North Seventy six Degrees East seventy six Poles near to a white oak South twenty five Degrees East forty one Poles to a locust Stake North thirty six Degrees East fifty eight Poles to two smal Hicorys south fifty five ½ Degrees East one Hundred and Thirty six poles to the Creek near a sycemore [sic] and thorn thence down the Creek the several courses to a walnut to his B^r Isaces [sic] line North fifty four Degrees West two hundred and forty Poles to two small white oak North thirty one Degrees East sixteen Poles to a black oak

Saplin on the old lin * * * with all Houses
Buildings orchards wayes water Courses Profits
Commoditys Hereditaments and appurtenances
whatsoever to the Said Premises hereby granted
or any part thereof Belonging or in any wise appertaining and the Reversion and Reversions
Remainder and Remainders Rents Issues &
Profits thereof and also all the Estate Right Title
use Trust Property or Claim or Demand whatsoever of him the Said Abraham Lincolen of In
and to the Said Premises and all Deeds Evidences and writings Touching or In any wise
Concerning the same To HAVE AND TO HOLD the
land hereby conveyed and all and Singular other
the Premises hereby Bargained and sold and Every Part and Parcle thereof with their and every
of their appurtenances unto the said man Michal
shanks His Heirs and assigns for Ever to the
only proper use and Behoof of them Michal
Shanks and of his heirs and assigns for ever and
the Said Abraham Lincolen and Bashaba his wife
for them selves theire Heirs and assigns by these
Presents Ab^m Lincolen and his wife at the time
of the Sealing and Delivery of these Presents
is Seized of a good Sure Perfect and Indefeazable Estate of Inheritance In fee Simple of and
In the said premises Hereby Granted and he
Hath good Power and Lawfull and absolute
right and authority to grant and Convey the
same to the said Michal Shanks In manner and
form aforsaid and that the premises now are and
so for ever hereafter shall remain and be free
and clear of and from all former and other Gifts

Grants Bargains Sales rights titles of Dowers
Dower Judgments Executions Titles Troubles
Charges and Incumberances whatsoever Made
done Commited or Suffred By the said Ab^m
Lincolen and Basheba his wife or any other person or persons whatsoever the assement [assess-
ment] hereafter to grow dwe [due] and Payable to the Collectors for the Time being for the
use of the Commonwealth of Virginia for' and
In Prospect of the Said Premises only Excepted
and forprized and the said Ab^m Lincolen and
Bathsheba his wife and theire Heirs all and singular the Premises hereby granted with the appurtenances unto the said Michal shanks His heirs
and assigns against them the said Ab^m Lincolen
and Bathshaba his weife [sic] and theire heirs and
all and Every other Person [or] Persons whatsoever shall and will Warrent and for Ever Defend
by these Presents and Lastly that the said Ab^m
Lincolen and Bathshabe his weife and theire Heirs
and Every other Person or Persons and theire
Heirs any thing having and Claiming In the
Premises herein before mentioned or Intended to
be hereby Bargained and sold shall and will from
time to time and at all Times hereafter at the
Reasonable Request and at the proper cost and
charges in the Laue of them the Said Michal
shanks His heirs or assigns make do and Execute or Procure to be made done and Executed
all and Ewery such further and other Reasonable
Act and acts thing or things Conveyances and
assurances for theire further Better and more
Effectual, Conveying and Assuring the Premises

SIGNATURE OF ABRAHAM AND BATHSEBA LINCOLN, GRANDFATHER AND GRANDMOTHER OF PRESIDENT LINCOLN

aforsaid with their and Every of their appurtenances unto the said Michal Shanks His Heirs and assigns as by the said Abraham Lincolen his heirs or assignes or their councils Learned in the Laue shall be Reasonable advised Devised or Required in Witness whereof the said Abraham Lincolen and Bathsheba his weufe [sic] Hath Hereunto set theire hand and seal the day & year first above written

Ab^m Lincoln
Batseb Lincon

Seal'd and Deliver'd
In Presence of

Charles Mair
Solomon Mathews
George Chrisman

At a court held for Rockingham County the 26 Day of June 1780 This Deed of Bargain & Sale from Abraham Lincoln & Bersheba his Wife to Michael Shanks was proved by the Oath of Charles Mair & George Chrisman & by the Solemn affirmation of Solomon Mathews the witnesses thereto and ordered to be recorded by the Court. Pet'. Hog C. R. C.

This sale was made about the time Abraham Lincoln purchased land in Kentucky. The next record we have of him is found in the Land Office of Larue County, Kentucky. The original grant is reproduced here and shows the form "Linkhorn" which has given rise to the theory of the German origin of Lincoln. Abraham Lincoln soon went with his family, including his son Thomas, the father of the President, to settle in Kentucky (then a part of Virginia).

The following additional land transactions of the Lincolns are recorded in the deed books of Harrisonburg, Virginia, before 1802:

> Grantee Jacob Lincoln, Aug. 28, 1778, Grantor Tunis Vanpelt, book OO, p. 344.
>
> Grantor Isaac Lincoln, Apr. 24, 1779, Grantee John Kring (?), book OOO, p. 345.
>
> Grantor Isaac Lincoln, Apr. 24, 1779, Grantee Philip Rimel (?), book OOO, p. 345.
>
> Grantee John Lincoln, Apr. 28, 1787, Grantors John Thomas et ux., book OO, p. 362.
>
> Grantee John Lincoln, Sept. 28, 1790, Grantor Robert Harrison, book OO, p. 371.
>
> Grantors Thomas Lincoln et ux., July 25, 1791, Grantee Jacob Lincoln, book OOO, 373.
>
> Grantee John Lincoln, Apr. 28, 1794, Grantor Henry Whisler, book OO, p. 25.
>
> Grantee John Lincoln, June 28, 1796, Grantors Henry Nave et ux., book OO, p. 160.
>
> Grantee John Lincoln, Oct. 28, 1796, Grantor Jacob Casner, book OO, p. 181.
>
> Grantee Jacob Lincoln, Oct. 16, 1797, Grantors Thomas Vance et ux., book OO, p. 252.
>
> Grantee Jacob Lincoln, July 16, 1798, Grantor Thomas Leach, book OO, p. 298.
>
> Grantors John Lincoln et ux., June 21, 1801, Grantee John Raider, book OOO, p. 433.

The following early epitaphs were found in the old Lincoln Burying Ground on Linville Creek:

To the | Memory | of | Jacob Lincoln Sr who was born on the 18th | day of November 1751

PRESENT VIEW OF LINVILLE'S CREEK WHERE IT PASSES THROUGH THE
ORIGINAL LINCOLN TRACTS.

and | departed this life on the | 20th day of February 1822 | aged 71 years 9 Months | and 2 days. Sacred | to the Memory of | John Lincoln | who departed this life | on the 13th [?] day of July 1818 | aged 35 years | and 5 months and 4 days.

Abraham Lincoln | Born March 15 | 1799 | Died June 18. 1851 | Aged 52 years 2 mo's | & 29 days.

It will thus appear that the interests of the Lincolns in the Linville Creek Region were extensive. Later it was complicated by the arrival of other members of the Lincoln family from Pennsylvania. Mordecai Lincoln, son of Mordecai the elder of Exeter, settled in Union Township, Fayette County, and died there in 1812. Most of his children seem to have gone to settle in the Valley of Virginia. Michael Lincoln, the son of Thomas, son of Mordecai, the elder, of Exeter, settled in Buffalo Valley. Hananiah Lincoln, son of Mordecai of Exeter, after serving in the 12th Pennsylvania Regiment in the Revolution, joined Daniel Boone's settlement in Kentucky, Sarah Lincoln, daughter of Mordecai of Exeter, married Joshua Davis, of the Juniata Valley.

CHAPTER VIII.

THE FORMS OF THE NAME LINCOLN.

The argument in support of the theory that Abraham Lincoln was sprung from a German family by the name of Linkhorn (written also Lincorn, Linckorn, Linckhorn), was based primarily upon this supposable German form of the name, and, secondly, upon the fact that Abraham Lincoln, the President of the United States, was descended from a family of that name in Berks County, Pennsylvania. It will now be in place to discuss the validity of this argument in the light of the documents already presented in the foregoing pages.

The documents relating to the Lincoln family, ranging all the way from Massachusetts to Kentucky, exhibit the following well authenticated forms of the name Lincoln. In Masachusetts we find "Lincoln," "Lincoen," a form in Abraham Lincoln's direct line. In the New Jersey documents we find "Lincoln," "Lincon," "Lincen," "Lincorn," Linckorn." In Pennsylvania we find "Lincoln," "Linkcoln," "Lincolin," "Lincorn," "Lingorn," "Linkorn," "Linkoln," "Linkoon." In Maryland we find "Lincoln," "Lincolne," "Linckhorn." In Virginia we find "Lincoln," "Lincolen," "Lincon." In Kentucky we find "Lincoln," "Linkhorn." Thus summing up the important forms we have the fol-

MARRIAGE CERTIFICATE OF THOMAS LINCOLN AND NANCY HANKS.
(By the Courtesy of Col. R. T. Durrett.)

lowing: *Lincoln, Lincolne, Lincolen, Linkcoln, Lincon, Lincoen, Lincen, Linckon, Linkon, Linkhoon, Linkorn, Linkhorn.* In addition to these forms of the name, that of "Linton" also has been considered as synonymous with "Lincoln," but as it seems, only sporadically, if at all.

As we have seen, the name and family of Lincoln have been traced back to New England and thence back to Old England, to the neighborhood of Hingham, whence a number of the New England settlers came to Massachusetts and here formed a settlement, which likewise was called Hingham. The name Lincoln itself is one of frequent occurrence in English records, and is applied both to persons and to places. It is usually derived from the two words *Lind* and *Colonia,* which as a compound, under the laws of euphonic change, would give *Lincolonia* and *Lincolne* or *Lincoln.*

The correct and, at the same time, the most persistent form of the name is *Lincoln.* All the other forms are but natural variations in the speech of the people or in the orthography of the scribe. There seems to be no evidence that any of the forms of the name are of German origin. The form which gave rise to the theory of Lincoln's German ancestry was, of course, *Linkhorn* and its variations, which occur, as we have seen, over almost the entire territory through which the family migrated.

In order to make the argument clearer, let us examine the various forms of the name and their iden-

tity, from the philological point of view. The form
Lincolne explains itself, as a variant spelling quite
common in the colonial and earlier records. The
form *Linkoln* is simply a more phonetic spelling
with "k" instead of hard "c." The form *Linkolen*
is the same form with the liquid made more vocalic
by the addition of an "e" before the "n," which is
a very common characteristic of the folkspeech. The
form *Lincoin* or *Lincoen* is simply a vocalization of
the liquid "l," which is also a common phonetic phenomenon. The forms *Lincon, Linckon, Linkon,* all
represent the same sound and exhibit a form of the
name in which the liquid has become silent and thus
dropped in the pronunciation as well as in the
orthography—also a well-known phenomenon in the
folkspeech. The pseudo-German forms, *Linkhorn,
Linkorn, Lincorn,* which seem to offer the most diffi-
culty, are really very simple, well authenticated phonetic changes which are found in the literatures and
are still going on in the speech of both Germanic and
Romanic peoples, namely, the simple interchange of
liquids, in this case the substitution of *r* for *l.*
Thus we see that all of the forms of the name *Lincoln* are natural variants, entirely in keeping with the
traditions of English speech and orthography.

Having disposed of the pseudo-German form of
the name, let us consider the occurrence of it outside
of the Lincoln family. If the presumable German
forms, *Linkorn, Lincorn,* etc., were German, we
should naturally expect to find them occurring as

MARRIAGE BOND AND CERTIFICATE OF THOMAS LINCOLN.
(By Courtesy of Col. R. T. Durrett.)

Lincoln, which is the normal form recognized by the scribe in this document, and the form Lincen or Lincon.

The other document mentioned above furnishes the clinching argument for the identity of the supposed German form of the name with the usual English form, *Lincoln*. The document in question is a deed recorded in City Hall, Philadelphia, bearing date April 4, 1794, and conveying land from Philip Price and Hannah, his wife, of Kingsessing Township, Philadelphia County, to Abraham Linckhorn, of the same township. This document contains the following notable passage:

"N. B. The surname of the second party to this Indenture has been mispelled through Misinformation to the Scrivener, tho commonly pronounced as it is speled above, it is written Lincoln."

Thus the name Lincoln, like the family, is not German but English. The tradition which has taken such a hold upon the German American mind as to give rise even to German poetry on Abraham Lincoln as a German, must be considered as without historic foundation.

CHAPTER IX.

THE LINCOLN MIGRATION TYPICALLY AMERICAN.

One of the most important results of geneological research in this country is, or should be, the new light shed upon colonization and settlement in America and the motives prompting migration to new lands. It will appear from the foregoing researches that the Lincoln family is one of the most typical and significant in American history.

The motive prompting the migration of the Lincolns through the various provinces reflects in each instance an important fact in the history of our early settlements. In the first movement of the Lincolns from Hingham and other parts of England, they were prompted by the widespread desire to seek a more favorable sphere of activity in the new world. They formed part of a larger company of emigrants who acquired land in the colony of Massachusetts. It was one of those concerted emigrations from a particular locality in the Old World with the purpose of making a compact settlement in the new land beyond the sea.

It can be clearly seen that the Lincoln family, like most large families, represented a variety of occupations. One was a yeoman, another a miller, another a weaver, all alert to the opportunities of improving their several trades in the new environment. So we have Thomas Lincoln, the yeoman or husbandman, Thomas Lincoln, the miller, Samuel Lincoln, the weaver, or at least the hired-man, or, probably more exactly, the apprentice of a weaver. As subsequent events indicate, the blacksmith trade was doubtless understood and practiced by some of the family.

It is the trade and industry of working iron which seems to furnish a clue to the motive of the sons of Mordecai Lincoln of Hull in their migration from Massachusetts to New Jersey. Their father, Mordecai of Hull, had already become an important factor in the iron industry of Massachusetts, having, as we have seen, a considerable share in the erection of the iron works at Bound Brook, Massachusetts, and having brought the iron industry to the highest point of perfection in the colony at that time by building a catalan forge for making wrought iron. It is significant that Mordecai Lincoln and Abraham, his brother, sons of Mordecai of Hull, migrated to that part of New Jersey in which iron had been found—the Red Bank region—evidently with the expectation that they might be able to develop the iron industry in New Jersey. In addition to their interests in iron, they naturally acquired land in the new settlement and became important landowners as well as ironmongers. We find Mordecai Lincoln mentioned later as ironmonger in Pennsylvania, and Abraham we find designated as "blacksmith", in addition to their occupation as yeomen.

OLD LINCOLN CABIN.
'EAR SPRINGFIELD, WASHINGTON COUNTY. KY

(By the Courtesy of Mr. Thomas B. Kirpatrik, of Hodgenville, Ky.)

It is therefore, more than a simple accident, or coincidence, that we find Mordecai Lincoln taking up land later in the French Creek region, that part of Pennsylvania in which the iron industry was developing and in which he erects a forge and carries on extensive iron operations, thus deserving the appellation of "ironmonger" in the old deed. In the case of Abraham, who settled in Springfield Township, Chester County, Pennsylvania, other motives may have operated to determine the place of his settlement. In the early land records of Philadelphia County, we find the name Saltar before 1700, showing that the Saltars had purchased land in Pennsylvania. As Mordecai Lincoln had married Hannah Saltar, it is quite likely that his attention, as well as that of his brother, Abraham, had been directed by the Saltar connections to the counties of Philadelphia and Chester, and that both might have settled nearer Philadelphia but for the fact that Mordecai wished to carry on the industry of mining and smelting iron, and so sought out the region of iron deposits along French Creek.

In the case of the sons of Mordecai Lincoln, the elder, of Exeter, Pennsylvania, son of Mordecai of Hull, Massachusetts, we find some of the old traditional trades re-appearing, as for example in John Lincoln, who is mentioned in the land record as "Weaver", showing that he had the trade of the great-great grandfather Samuel Lincoln, the weaver-apprentice and immigrant in Massachusetts.

The migration of the Lincolns from Pennsylvania to Virginia and other parts of the South and West, reflects one of the most important movements of American population—the movement along the Great Valley and across the mountains into the valleys of the Ohio and the Mississippi. It is along this route that the migration of the Lincolns moved from Berks County, Pennsylvania.

As early as 1710, the Swiss and Palatine Germans under the guidance of De Graffenried settled at New Bern, North Carolina, but were soon afterward attacked by the Indians and massacred or dispersed. The survivors took refuge in Virginia and formed a settlement at Germanna in 1714. The eyes of the Virginians had already been opened a hundred years before to the excellent qualities of the German settlers as artisans and farmers. Governor Spottswood now encouraged the Palatines to settle on his lands. Even before 1720 the provincial council of Virginia had devoted special attention to a general plan of settling Palatines in the uplands of Virginia.

In this year, 1720, John van Meter, a trader from the Hudson River region in New York, made a prospecting tour through the South Branch region of Virginia. 1727 Isaac van Meter, the son of John, visited the same region of Virginia. Meanwhile, isolated settlers seem to have taken up land in the Valley of Virginia. Adam Miller appears to have settled there near Massanutting in 1726 or 1727. In the year 1730, Isaac van Meter, and John his brother, sons of the elder John, received patents of

THE CABIN IN WHICH ABRAHAM LINCOLN, THE PRESIDENT, WAS BORN, FEBRUARY 12, 1809.

land from Governor Gouch, of Virginia. John van Meter patented 10,000 acres at the forks of the Shenandoah (Sherando or Shenando) and Cedar Creek, Cedar Lick and Strong Lick, and 20,000 acres farther below. Isaac van Meter patented 10,000 acres in the lower valley.

In the year 1728 a serious event turned the attention of Pennsylvania settlers toward Virginia. In this year the Indians made a hostile attack upon the settlement of Falkner Swamp and Goschenhoppen. The settlers of Cold Brook Dale sent a petition to Governor Gordon, of Pennsylvania, asking him to protect them against the savages. Many of the settlers, feeling insecure in Pennsylvania, began to look for more favorable conditions in other provinces, and naturally turned their eyes in the direction of Maryland and Virginia, toward which settlers were beginning to move along the eastern slopes of the Blue Ridge.

In the year 1732 Jost Hite (Justus Heid), a native of Strassburg in Elsass, purchased land of the Van Meters on the Opequon Creek and settled some sixteen families from Lancaster County, Pennsylvania. Among the names of these settlers were, George Bowman, Jacob Chrisman, Paul Froman (all three sons-in-law of Hite), Robert McKay, William Duff and Peter Stephen. They took the route of the old Monocacy Road, by way of Harper's Ferry, and settled five miles to the north of the present Winchester. In 1733 Jacob Stauffer (or Stover) received a grant of 5000 acres of land in

the Gerando (Shenando) region, farther up the
valley, toward the present site of Harrisonburg. The
old name of Strasburg, was Staufferstadt, and per-
petuated the name of this early settler. In 1736
Peter Bowman appears among the settlers, and in
1738 Peter Franciscus. In 1746 we find William
Lenivell (or Linvill) taking up land along the Linville Creek, which now bears his name.

A glance at the names of these early settlers in
the Valley of Virginia, and the references in the
land records show that many of them came from
what was old Lancaster County, Pennsylvania (including later Lancaster, York and Lebanon). The
earlier names, like "Bowman", "Franciscus",
"Funk", point directly to the early settlers in the
Pequea region of Lancaster County (then Chester
County) of 1710. Likewise the name "Lenivell"
or "Linvill" is one of frequent occurrence in Lancaster County, covering entire pages of the old deed
books in the Recorder's office.

The contact between John Lincoln and this early
migration to Virginia is twofold. In the first place
John Lincoln owned land in Caernarvon Township,
Lancaster County, as well as in Amity and Union,
Berks County, and naturally came into touch with
the residents of that region who were migrating to
Virginia. In the second place he had a special
instance of such migration in his adventurous
neighbor and friend, Daniel Boone, of Oley.

Daniel Boone, of Oley, had set out with his
father and kinsman from Berks County, Pennsyl-

vania, in 1750, with a view to settling in the Great Valley. They took the usual route by Harper's Ferry and passed up the Shenandoah Valley. Tradition says—in this instance it doubtless reflects history—that the Boones tarried a while on Linville Creek, six miles north of Harrisonburg, Virginia. In the following year, 1751, the Boones pressed on through the Valley of Virginia to the Yadkin region, where Squire Boone, Daniel's father, chose a claim at Buffalo Lick, at the junction of Dutchman's Creek and the north point of the Yadkin.

The ties of friendship between the Lincolns and the Boones in Berks County were drawn closer by the marriage of Abraham Lincoln, the posthumous son of Mordecai, the elder, of Exeter, to Anna Boone, July the 10th, 1760. It was thus natural that John Lincoln, or "Virginia John", as he was later called, and his kinsmen should be informed of the wanderings of the Boones in the Great Valley. Thus the motive of John Lincoln's migration to Virginia is easily found. He, unlike the other sons of Mordecai Lincoln, the elder, of Exeter, was not attached to the soil of Pennsylvania by inheritance but by the purchase of land, having received his part of his father's estate in New Jersey, and afterwards sold it for cash. Then, too, the opportunities of acquiring large tracts of land in the Valley of Virginia at a moderate price, and the fact that his kinsmen and neighbors, the Boones, had already migrated thither furnished further incentive.

The exact date of John Lincoln's migration from
Berks County, Pennsylvania, to Augusta County,
Virginia, cannot be fixed, but it must have been
between 1765, the year in which John Lincoln's
name ceases to appear in the tax lists of Berks
County, and 1768, the year in which he appears as
a resident of Augusta County, Virginia. As we have
seen he sold the major part of his land in Pennsylvania between the years 1763 and 1765. It is quite
likely that he went to Virginia in 1765 or 1766, and
like the Boones tarried in the Linville Creek region
until he could decide upon a place of residence.
Instead of following the Boones on to the Yadkin,
he purchased land on Linville Creek from the
McKays (or McCoys) and others who had received
an original grant. As the land records show, John
Lincoln later in life conveyed his land to his sons.

It will be remembered that Daniel Boone set out
from North Carolina for Transylvanian Virginia,
that region which is now known as Kentucky. In
1773 the Boones, with their families, left the Yadkin
to settle in the land then recently explored by Daniel
Boone, and met with the disastrious massacre in the
Cumberland Gap. Meanwhile this region, which
had been entered twenty years before by Governor
Spottswood, now attracted the attention of the
Washingtons—George Washington and his brothers
—of the Lees, and even of Benjamin Franklin.
Hundreds of settlers began to pour in through the
Ohio Valley, and founded the town of Louisville.

DEED SHOWING THE CORRECT NAME OF "LINCOLN," NOT "LINKHORN."
(Original in City Hall, Philadelphia.)

Land-Office Treasury WARRANT, No 3334

To the principal Surveyor of any County within the Commonwealth of Virginia:

THIS shall be your WARRANT to Survey and lay off in one or more Surveys, for *Abraham Linkhorn* his Heirs or Assigns, the Quantity of *four hundred* Acres of Land, due unto the said *Abraham Linkhorn* in Consideration of the Sum of *one hundred & sixty pounds* current Money paid into the publick Treasury; the Payment whereof to the Treasurer hath been duly certified by the Auditors of publick Accounts, and their Certificate received into the Land Office. GIVEN under my Hand, and the Seal of the said Office, on this *fourth* Day of *March* in the Year One Thousand Seven Hundred and *eighty*.

S. Carr D. R. d. O.

WARRANT ISSUED TO ABRAHAM LINCOLN, IN KENTUCKY, SHOWING THE NAME "LINKHORN."

Early in the year 1780, three hundred so-called family boats are said to have arrived at the Falls of the Ohio. The Legislature of Virginia passed laws for the protection and encouragement of the new settlers.

Naturally, the cismontane Virginians were eager to seize the opportunity of acquiring new fertile lands at the normal price of forty cents per acre. It was in the midst of this rush for land in the Ohio Valley, in the year 1780, that Abraham Lincoln, of Linville Creek, Virginia, purchased four hundred acres of land in Transylvanian Virginia, for the sum of $160, and soon afterwards, having disposed of his land on Linville Creek, as we have already seen from the old deed, set out for the Valley of the Ohio. The original warrant for this purchase of four hundred acres, is here reproduced in fac-simile and will speak for itself. The survey is dated May 7, 1785.

In addition to this purchase, Abraham Lincoln owned other lands in Kentucky. According to the researches made by Colonel Reuben T. Durrett, of Louisville, Kentucky, Abraham Lincoln owned the following tracts of land in that region:

1. A tract containing four hundred acres, on Long Run, a branch of Floyd's Fork, in Jefferson County, entered May 29th, 1780.

2. A tract of eight hundred acres on Green River, near Green River Lick, entered June 7th, 1780.

3. A tract of five hundred acres in Campbell County, surveyed September 27, 1798, and patented June 30th, 1799, but taken up before his death in 1784.

The tract of 500 acres, entered by Daniel Boone in his Field Book, would seem to indicate still another purchase of land in the present Kentucky by Abraham Lincoln. The warrant is No. 5994 and Boone's survey entry is dated December 11, 1782. A fac-simile may be found in Nicolay and Hay's *Abraham Lincoln.*

The tradition that Abraham Lincoln went to North Carolina is doubtless a reminiscence of the route which he took to his newly acquired lands in the present State of Kentucky. He followed naturally Boone's Wilderness Road, and probably joined a company of settlers going that way at the time.

Thus we have followed the Lincolns in their wanderings to the West, that region now known as Kentucky, then still a part of the old territory of Virginia. Abraham Lincoln was killed, as tradition has it, in 1784, by the Indians, while at work with his sons, Mordecai, Josiah and Thomas, in the clearings. The older boys ran for help, Mordecai to the house for the gun, and Josiah to the fort for men. Mordecai returned with the gun in time to shoot the Indian who was just about to scalp his six-year-old brother, Thomas. This Thomas was the father of Abraham Lincoln, the President of the United States.

It was the irony of American migration which

Surveyed for Abraham Linkhorn 400 acres of Land in Jefferson County by virtue of a Treasury Warrant No 3334 on the Fork of Floyds Fork now called the Long Run beginning about two miles up the said Fork from the Mouth of a Fork of the same formerly called Tes Fork at a Sugar Tree standing on the side of the same marked SB and extending thence East 300 poles to a Poplar and Sugar Tree North 213⅓ poles to a Beech and Dogwood West 300 poles to a White Oak and Hickory South 213⅓ poles to the Beginning — May 7th 1785   William Shanon DSJC
Chenaniah Lincoln and,   William May SJC
Josiah Lincoln C C }
Abraham Linkhorn Markers

SURVEY OF THE FIRST WARRANT OF LAND TO ABRAHAM LINCOLN IN
KENTUCKY (THEN VIRGINIA).

reared the great emancipator of the slaves on the Blue Grass soil of Kentucky. Abraham Lincoln was in a peculiar sense the heir of all the great American traditions. Sprung from an English family, which had been inured to the hardships of New England, tarried among the early Dutch and English settlers of East Jersey, taken root and thrown among the Germans and Quakers of Pennsylvania, shared the adventures and perils of the frontier life of Virginia and Kentucky, Abraham Lincoln was the best example of that sturdy, fearless American citizenship, great not because he made far-seeing plans of self-glorification, but because he possessed that inherent heroism and devotion to duty which prepared him for all emergencies, even those of civil war, and won for him the enduring names of Emancipator of American Slaves and Martyr President of the Republic of Freemen.

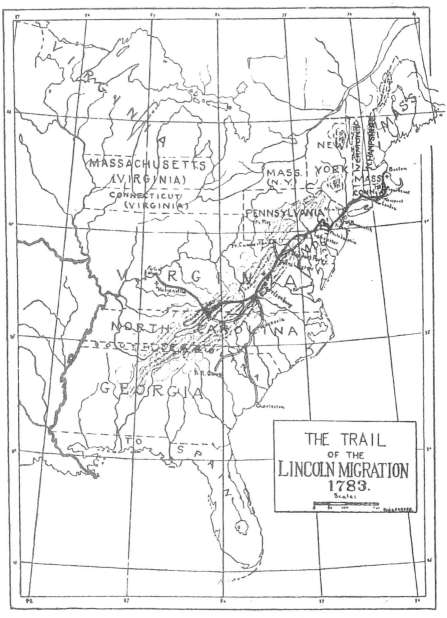

MAP OF THE MIGRATION OF THE LINCOLNS FROM HINGHAM, MASS., TO KENTUCKY.
The Marks X Indicates Hingham, Mass., Red Bank, N. J., Coventry, Pa.,
Linville's Creek, Va., and Hodgenville, Ky.

INDEX OF LINCOLNS REFERRED TO IN THIS WORK

Part Three - Appendix

152

After presenting a paper on the German heritage of the Ohio Valley at a conference at the University of Louisville, a member of the audience asked whether it was true that Daniel Boone was of German descent, and whether the original spelling of his name had been the German name "Bohne." I replied that I had never heard of this, but promised to investigate the matter.

Thus was my interest in Daniel Boone renewed, since as a boy I had been greatly interested in Boone, Davy Crockett, and other frontiersmen. After arriving in Lexington to do graduate study at the University of Kentucky, one of the first places I chose to visit was Boonesborough. Subsequently, I obtained a position at the University of Cincinnati, where I became the Curator of the German-Americana Collection, a veritable gold mine of information with regard to the German heritage of the U.S., especially in the Ohio Valley. (1)

After returning from my Louisville presentation, I checked several sources in the German-Americana Collection, and quickly established that Boone was not of German, but of English descent, but also learned how inextricably he was connected to the German heritage, and what the basis was for the notion that he was of German descent. (2)

The legends surrounding the assertion that Boone was of German stock revolved around four factors:

1. Birthplace: Boone was born in a Pennsylvania German county.

2. Name: There were Germans in Pennsylvania who spelled their name in the following forms: Bohne, Bohny, and Boone.

3. Bilingualism: Boone was an English-German bilingual.

4. Kentucky's German heritage: German-Americans, especially from Pennsylvania, played a prominent role in the settlement not only of Kentucky, but figured noticeably in the settlement of Boonesborough.

5. German Interest in Boone: The interest in Boone in Germany was reflected in several publications, beginning in the 1780s.

All of these factors require that further light be shed on them, since they are not generally well known.

First, with regard to Boone's birth place, it should be noted that Boone's family arrived from England in Philadelphia, Pennsylvania in 1717. At that time, the colony of Pennsylvania had already become the center of the German immigration and settlement, and both the German and Anglo elements were equal in size (each composing one-third of the population). Moreover, the Boone family moved to Berks County, which to this day is noted for its Pennsylvania German heritage. Here there were not only the German Mennonites, but also the Amish, the German Baptist Brethren, or Dunkards, and the German Moravians. (3)

Boone was born in 1734 in Oley Township (now Exeter) in Berks County, and hence grew up in a German-speaking community, so that it was not surprizing that he early on became bilingual. This may have been enforced by the fact that he was basically educated at home, since as a German Lutheran minister noted in 1748, there were no schools in Oley, stating "In Oley sind die Schulen entfernt." (4) In 1742, Count von Zinzendorf, the German Moravian missionary, held a church synod in one of the Oley barns, and held a church synod in one of the Oley barns, and since the Moravians were active in their missioanry work on the frontier, several Delaware Indians from the frontier were involved. Hence, it can be said that the German Moravians contributed in part to his earliest contacts with Indians and the frontier. (5)

Second, with regard to his name, the question was raised about the German ancestry of Boone because of the similarity of the name with the German names Bohne and Bony. This confusion was rendered all that more understandable, for example, in the case of Andreas Bohny, a German immigrant who arrived in Philadelphia in 1729. His descendants spelled their name "Boone," which resulted in there actually being a Boone family line in Pennsylvania which was of German descent. (6) This name similarity, hence, contributed to the German ancestry legend.

Third, Boone was also thought to have been of German descent because of his English-German bilingualism. As noted earlier, this was not surprizing since he was born and raised in a German-speaking community. As early as 1857, one commentator wrote that it was because of his origins in Berks County and his ability to speak German "that he was supposed to be a Dutchman, or of German extraction." (7)

The fourth factor pertained to Kentucky's German heritage. Germans not only played a prominent role in the early exploration and settlement of Kentucky, they accompanied Boone on his ventures there, and were amongst the early settlers at Boonesborough. (8) Indeed, when Boone in 1774 was chose to lead the surveying party for the Transylvania Company which aimed to found a settlement in Kentucky, he was accompanied by his lifelong Pennsylvania German friend, Michael Steiner (also known as Stoner). The latter was described as "a large strong dutchman" and "one of the numerous Pennsylvania Germans" who came to Kentucky with other Pennsylvanians. (9)

The fifth factor pertains to the strong interest there was in Germany, which was reflected in several publications. In 1785 a German journal first published adventure stories dealing with Daniel Boone. The editor of the journal remarked that since so little was known about the American interior, that Boone's adventure stories would certainly fill the gap. These stories were actually excerpts of

Boone's so-called autobiography contained in John Filson's book dealing with the discovery of Kentucky - that a German translation appeared only a year after the English-language edition (1784) is an indication of the German interest not only in America, but also in Daniel Boone. (10)

Such German-language publications attracted the interest of prospective immigrants, especially to the Ohio Valley. However, it would be a book, published in 1829 by Gottfried Duden, which is considered the most widely read and influential single book in the history of the German immigration to America, which also has a "Boone dimension." (11)

Duden in the 1820s came to the U.S., travelled throughout the Midwest, and settled in Missouri, and upon his return to Germany, published his book about America in 1829. This book exerted a tremendous influence on the German immigration, as many were influenced to settle not only in the Midwest, but many specifically chose to go to Missouri, some wanting to settle in exactly the same county where Duden had been.

What was the connection between Duden and Boone, which further demonstrates the German dimension of interest and fascination in the frontiersman? As noted, the German interest in Boone was already quite strong by the 1820s, so it is not surprizing that when Duden came to Missouri in 1825, he chose to acquire land and live in an area "predominantly settled by the Boone clan and their Kentucky friends." Boone, it should be remembered had moved west after he felt that Kentucky was becoming to filled up with settlers. Duden's farm was located eight miles from the farm of Nathan Boone, the son of Daniel Boone, which was located on the Osage Woman River. Not only did Duden settle in Missouri Boone country, he became well acquainted with Nathan Boone, a state surveyor, and they travelled and hunted together in Missouri. In his book Duden wrote respectfully of Boone "who has become so famous in the cultural history of America and whose name is used to designate various places." However, he does note that "in Europe tales have been spread about him that have no foundation in fact." (12)

Duden "acquired much of his information about homesteading, pioneer life, and related subjects from these transplanted Kentucky pioneers." This accounts in part for Duden's "frequent references to the almost complete self-sufficiency of pioneer farming, the ease with which the whole process could be accomplished, and the joys of living in a virtual paradisiacal wilderness." (13)

It is, hence, interesting to note that Boone contributed not only to the Pennsylvania German settlement of Kentucky, but that the continued German interest in him, as evidenced especially by the Duden book, would contribute to further German immigration and settlement through the Ohio Valley directed to Missouri. Although not of German descent, the German-American dimensions surrounding Boone contributed to the interest which I already had in him, and led me to explore the question of Lincoln's ancestry, when this question arose.

The questions surrounding both Boone and Lincoln are another indication of the degree to which America has been influenced by the German heritage. Although neither was of German descent, the influence of the German heritage on their family can clearly be seen. Indeed, it was so evident was it, that the question of German ancestry emerged as a logical possibilitiy.

Notes:

1. See Don Heinrich Tolzmann, *Catalog of the German-Americana Collection, University of Cincinnati*, (Muenchen: K.G. Saur, 1990).

2. See H.A. Rattermann, "Die deutschen Pioniere von Lexington, Kentucky," *Der Deutsche Pionier*, 10(1878): 273-78.

3. See John Bakeless, *Master of the Wilderness: Daniel Boone*, (New York: William Morrow Company, 1939), pp. 4-5.

4. Bakeless, p. 10.

5. With regard to the German Moravians on the frontier, see Don Heinrich Tolzmann, *The First Description of Cincinnati and other Ohio Settlements: The Travel Report of Johann Heckewelder, 1792*, (Lanham, Maryland: University Press of America, 1988).

6. Rattermann, p. 273.

7. Rattermann, p. 273.

8. For references to Kentucky's German heritage, see Tolzmann, volume 1, pp. 233-35. Also by the same author, see *The Ohio Valley German Biographical Index*, (Bowie, Maryland: Heritage Books, Inc. 1992).

9. For references to Steiner, see Bakeless, pp. 77-80, 85, 89, 151, 295, 347, and also, Rattermann, pp. 273-78.

10. See Don Heinrich Tolzmann, "The German Image of Cincinnati Before 1830," in: *German-Americana: Selected Essays*, (Bowie, Maryland: Heritage Books, Inc., forthcoming book).

11. See Gottfried Duden, *Report on a Journey to the Western States of North America*, (Columbia: University of Missouri Pr., 1980).

12. Duden, pp. 77-78.

13. Duden, p. 349.

Heritage Books by Don Heinrich Tolzmann:

Abraham Lincoln's Ancestry: German or English?
M. D. Learned's Investigatory History, with an Appendix on Daniel Boone

Amana: William Rufus Perkins' and Barthinius L. Wick's
History of the Amana Society, or Community of True Inspiration

Americana Germanica: Paul Ben Baginsky's
Bibliography of German Works Relating to America, 1493–1800

Biography of Baron Von Steuben, the Army of the American Revolution and
Its Organizer: Rudolf Cronau's Biography of Baron von Steuben

CD: German-American Biographical Index (Midwest Families)

CD: Germans, Volume 2

CD: The German Colonial Era (four volumes)

Cincinnati's German Heritage

Covington's German Heritage

Custer: Frederick Whittaker's Complete Life of General George A. Custer,
Major General of Volunteers, Brevet Major General U.S. Army
and Lieutenant-Colonel Seventh U.S. Cavalry

Dayton's German Heritage: Karl Karstaedt's Golden Jubilee
History of the German Pioneer Society of Dayton, Ohio

Early German-American Newspapers: Daniel Miller's History

German Achievements in America: Rudolf Cronau's Survey History

German Americans in the Revolution

German Immigration to America: The First Wave

German Pioneer Life and Domestic Customs

German Pioneer Lifestyle

German Pioneers in Early California: Erwin G. Gudde's History

German-American Achievements: 400 Years of Contributions to America

German-Americana in Europe: Two Guides to Materials Relating to
American History in the German, Austrian, and Swiss Archives

German-Americana: A Bibliography

Germany and America, 1450–1700

Kentucky's German Pioneers: H. A. Rattermann's History

Lives and Exploits of the Daring Frank and Jesse James: Thaddeus Thorndike's
Graphic and Realistic Description of Their Many Deeds of Unparalleled
Daring in the Robbing of Banks and Railroad Trains

Louisiana's German Heritage: Louis Voss' Introductory History

Maryland's German Heritage: Daniel Wunderlich Nead's History

Memories of the Battle of New Ulm: Personal Accounts of the Sioux Uprising.
L. A. Fritsche's History of Brown County, Minnesota (1916)

CPSIA information can be obtained
at www.ICGtesting.com
Printed in the USA
LVHW040127210420
654150LV00006B/1587